HOLY SCRIPTURE

Books by James Barr
Published by The Westminster Press

Holy Scripture:
  Canon, Authority, Criticism

The Scope and Authority of the Bible

Fundamentalism

HOLY SCRIPTURE

Canon, Authority, Criticism

JAMES BARR

THE WESTMINSTER PRESS
PHILADELPHIA

Published by The Westminster Press®
Philadelphia, Pennsylvania

PRINTED IN THE UNITED STATES OF AMERICA
9 8 7 6 5 4 3 2 1

Library of Congress Cataloging in Publication Data

Barr, James.
  Holy Scripture.

  Bibliography: p.
  Includes index.
  1. Bible—Canon. 2. Bible—Criticism, interpretation, etc.
I. Title.
BS465.B35 1983   220.1   82-20123
ISBN 0-664-21395-2
ISBN 0-664-24477-7 (pbk.)

Preface

THIS book is based upon the James Sprunt Lectures delivered in February 1982 at Union Theological Seminary, Richmond, Virginia, and in fact is very close to the text as then delivered, with only some additions and modifications. It was a great honour to be invited to lecture in this very distinguished series, and the lecturer benefited greatly from the stimulus of the intelligent and appreciative audience that Richmond provided. Thanks are due to the President of the Seminary, T. Hartley Hall IV, and to the entire Seminary community, but especially to the three professors of Old Testament there, James L. Mays, Patrick D. Miller Jr., and W. Sibley Towner, all of them close friends.

Material of this kind, however, requires a long gestation and a good deal of experiment; and in fact various versions of the same basic thoughts were presented by me in the Clark Lectures in Pomona College, California, in the spring of 1981; in the Laidlaw Lectures at Knox College, Toronto, also in the spring of 1981; and in the Sanderson Lectures at Ormond College, Melbourne, Australia, in 1982. I acknowledge with gratitude the encouragement and stimulus that was received through the opportunity to lecture on this and related subjects in these fine institutions. Many of the thoughts here expressed were also worked out in normal lecture courses given in the Divinity School of the University of Chicago in spring 1981 and in Oxford University in the same year. Discussion with students in these courses was most valuable and creative.

The discussions in this book are not intended to lead to any kind of final solution of problems, nor to a history of the question, and least of all to any hermeneutical programme which, once explained, can then be put into action. Only limited questions can be taken up within the space available here. In particular, no attempt is made to give any complete discussion of the matter of biblical authority. In such a respect this book may be read in conjunction with my other earlier books, in particular *Old and New in Interpretation* (1966, soon to be republished in a second edition), *The Bible in the Modern World* (1973) and *Explorations in Theology 7* (1980; American title *The Scope and Authority of the Bible*).

Christ Church
Oxford
February 1982

Contents

I

Before scripture and after scripture

THERE was not always a Bible. But when was the time that was 'before scripture', before there was a Bible? Clearly, in the misty antiquity of the human race, before Abraham, before the origins of Israel: then there was as yet no holy scripture. But it is not to this distant antiquity that I refer. When we say 'before scripture', we are speaking of the time of the Bible itself. In what we call 'biblical times', or in much of them, there was as yet no Bible.[1] The men of the Bible were, as we now see it, engaged in the process out of which our Bible in the end would emerge, but they themselves had no Bible: at that time, clearly, the Bible as we know it was not yet there. A scripture, in the sense of an already existing, defined and delimited, written guide for the religion, did not yet exist. In the time of (say) the prophet Isaiah there was as yet no such scripture, and he never speaks of there being one. St. Paul came to believe that Jesus was alive and was Lord, but not because he had read about it in any written Gospel. It is notorious that there is, in the earlier stages of Christianity, little or no appeal to the written accounts that we now know as the Gospels, or even to such previous written sources as may have gone into the production of them. Even if such written sources existed, the fact that so little mention is made of them, so little appeal made to them, seems to demonstrate that they had no quite central or decisive function in the religion: the religion could exist and expand without them.

Thus the time of the Bible was a time when the Bible was not yet there. It is ironic that we use the term 'biblical studies' to designate our work on this period. Biblical faith, the faith of the men of the Bible, was not in its own nature a scriptural religion. Faith and religion, within the Bible, were not faith

[1] I had already formulated this expression when I came across the similar thought of Patrick Henry, *New Directions in New Testament Study* (Philadelphia: Westminster, 1979), p. 41: 'Those who wrote the books of the New Testament had no New Testament'.

and religion defined and determined by a Bible. Only later, after scripture had been formed and delimited, after the Bible had come to be perceived as a complete, finished, and delimited entity, did it become natural or indeed possible to see and to define Christianity as a scriptural religion, a religion the shape of which was determined and controlled by a written holy book; and, with appropriate shifts of emphasis, the same may be said of Judaism. The Muslims later used the term *'ahl ul-kitāb*, 'People of the Book', to comprise those communities whose religion, at least as they, the Muslims, understood it, was defined and circumscribed by a particular scripture; and in this designation they included the Jews and the Christians, as well as themselves. Of themselves this was true from the beginning: from the commencement of Islam the Book was there. But in Judaism and in Christianity, in the long periods during which the material for the Book was being generated, the Jews and the Christians were not yet 'People of the Book'; and indeed it is doubtful whether either of them, and particularly the Christians, ever became People of the Book to the extent that the Muslims did. The men of the Bible, or most of them, lived in a time *before scripture*, before there was a Bible.

Many traditional doctrines of scripture, however, take their departure from the situation where the Bible is already complete, defined, known and acknowledged. The Bible is understood to be already *there*, it is already demarcated from other writings. This is so in both Catholic and Protestant doctrines but it is particularly evident in Protestantism because in it the role and the authority of scripture are more starkly isolated and more sharply defined as uniquely essential. Traditional doctrines—and most emphatically in Protestant orthodoxy—were from the start predicated upon the existence of scripture as a whole, as a collection delimited and defined. The canon of scripture, i.e. the list which defined which books lay within the scripture and, by exclusion, which books were not within it, was seen as complete, exclusive and unchanging; and the attributes of scripture, its inspiration, its necessity, its sufficiency, its perspicuity and so on, were applied in a more or less level way to all parts of the Bible. In Protestant orthodoxy scripture was taken to be the central criterion for faith and, even more, it was taken to be the central *source* for doctrine: thus doctrine was represented as if it derived from scripture, so that in the total scheme of understanding scripture had a place antecedent to doctrine. Doctrine, to be valid, must be seen to derive from scripture. Faith was required to be biblical, in the sense that its content had to be derivable from the sum of material of the entire holy scripture.

Moreover, because scripture was one body of material all of which alike uniquely came from God, and which had the same attributes throughout, its meaning was discerned through a process of complementation. Though inspiration was mentioned explicitly in only one or two places, the fact that it was mentioned at all was sufficient reason for its purport to be spread over the entire range of the Bible, while at the same time it was supposed that it did not apply to any non-canonical book. Though it was possible to write a Gospel which did not mention the Virgin Birth, the mention of it, where it *was* mentioned, was allowed to complement the non-mention of it elsewhere. Thus the Gospels were often studied through a Harmony, which added their contents together, rather than through a Synopsis, which would have made the differences between them more clear.

Now the strange thing was that, in thus taking its stand upon the canon as a complete entity, the church—and especially the Protestant branch of it—was actually taking its stand, to a considerable extent, outside the Bible rather than within it. To take completed scripture as the starting point was automatically to place the starting point outside the situation of biblical man. Completed scripture was something that was not there until a long time after the central events, after the time—if we may so call it—of biblical revelation was past: for the New Testament, one or two generations, perhaps more, and for the Old Testament, or almost all of it, some centuries.

There was thus a deep anachronism in the traditional doctrine. Looking as it did at the completed scripture, believed to be, through the operation of a unique inspiration, absolutely and qualitatively distinct from all other books and from all unwritten tradition, that doctrine focused not on the biblical period, when this complete scripture did not yet exist, but on a situation that obtained only after the biblical period was over. And yet on the other hand it could not and did not carry this out wholeheartedly and consequently: for it continued to revere the *persons* of the Bible—Moses, Isaiah, Jesus, St. Paul—and to see them in their own times and situation as far as limitations of historical perspective could permit, and to consider their teachings, attitudes, and actions as authoritative. Thus even traditional orthodoxy was not narrowly focused upon the scriptural text alone: it understood it through reference to the acting persons who wrote some of it and whose actions, teachings, and lives were told within it.

For the difference was not simply one of time but still more one of attitudes. These men of the Bible were in their own time, their own lives and thinking, not nearly so exclusively controlled by a fixed, delimited, and complete written scripture as Protestant believers were expected to be, indeed they were not exclusively controlled by scripture in this way at all. In imposing upon the Christian believer a form of faith understood to be strictly and exclusively controlled by scripture, Protestant orthodoxy was imposing upon him something that the men of the Bible, or most of them, had not known. Within the Bible itself religion was not a scriptural religion in the sense that it later, and especially after the Reformation, became normal to suppose. The actual relations between faith, creative originality, and the formation of traditions (eventually to become scripture) were different. In the Bible faith was not controlled by scripture: rather, scripture derived from faith. Thus the attitudes of passive acceptance of scriptural control, which Protestantism often inculcated into its people, were substantially different in quality from the attitudes which the men of the Bible themselves maintained. In this respect the traditional view of the Bible contained serious inner contradictions: in particular, it encouraged the reader to read into the words of scripture meanings that were not there at all.

It should be observed that the biblical evidence for all this does not depend on any 'critical' view or reconstruction but is available in the text of the Bible as it stands. Even if we use no historical analysis at all, it is apparent from the text of most of the Old Testament as it stands that the writers do not reckon with a written 'scripture' as a totally dominant, known, and acknowledged factor and force in the life of Israel. In this regard the evidence of the historical books and prophets seems to be decisive. The prophets, from Elijah and Elisha in the ninth century, through Amos, Hosea, Isaiah, and Micah in the eighth, and down to those like Zechariah, Haggai, and Malachi after the return from exile, spoke for God, and one of their key phrases was 'Thus says the Lord'; but they did not speak on the basis of an already existing scripture, they did not mention any such scripture, and there is no evidence that such material, conceived as a 'scripture', played a significant part in their minds. Rather, their speech was spontaneous, they spoke as God himself directly gave them speech. Old Testament man related to God much more through holy persons and institutions, and through a sort of direct personal and verbal communication with God, and little or not at all through pre-existing written and authoritative holy books.

David walked with the Lord, and Solomon is reputed to have gained great wisdom; and many of the later kings in Judah and Israel faced grave problems of good and evil, sin and repentance; but very seldom is anything said about any written books as a resource to which one might turn. Even of a pious king like Hezekiah (around 700 BC), who was anxious to do the right thing and to please his God, and who clearly did something to reform the religion in a direction which the Old Testament approved of, we do not hear that he read any books or consulted any; and it is the best part of a century later, around 622 BC, that Josiah king of Judah was told of the discovery of a 'book of the Torah' in the Temple, a book the reading of which greatly surprised and perturbed the king, so that he tore his clothes, consulted a prophetess for additional guidance and information, and read the book before the people, pledging them all to obey it. It was some time again after this, in the fourth year of Jehoiakim king of Judah, around 606 BC, that the word of the Lord came to Jeremiah and instructed him to take a scroll and write upon it all the words that he had spoken, against Israel, Judah, and all the nations, from the days of Josiah until then; and, after this scroll had been burned by the king, another was written in its place (Jer. 36).[2]

There is thus a great difference between the religion of the Old Testament, as it was for those who lived by it, and the idea of a religion controlled by scripture. One may ask why this difference has not been more often noticed. The reason may be as follows. The character of theological discussion has often been such that an emphasis on scripture, and an emphasis on direct revelation or communication, have been felt to count on the same side, *as far as concerns our modern discussion.* People think that reliance on a prophet and his words, and reliance on scripture, are the same sort of thing, broadly speaking: both are an appeal to an ancient authority, speaking articulately in words understood to come from God. It is felt, therefore, that they confirm each other reciprocally. And for our modern questions this may or may not be so. But in fact they are quite different things. Prophetic speech is personal and local; it may be recorded or may not, and it may be modified or may not;[3] unless it is fixed and made into scripture, it does not have permanent public accessibility. In respect of the question, what was the nature of the faith and religion of the men of the Bible, direct communication and scriptural religion are not on the same, but on opposite, sides.

Something should now be said about the Law of Moses. Is not this massive and imposing corpus a demonstration that Israel possessed a more or less fixed body of authoritative material which constituted more or less a scripture? And there is no reason to doubt the existence, within the Torah, of elements going back to an early date; indeed some of them, far from being first communicated by Moses, were probably

[2] Obviously it was not *normal* that prophetic sayings should be collected and written down, and it is interesting to consider why this was done with these older prophecies of Jeremiah. And why did he write down old prophecies, rather than speak a new oracle appropriate for a new and dangerous international situation? It is attractive to follow Douglas Jones: 'There can be little doubt that the motive which led Jeremiah to dictate the oracles of his life's ministry was to demonstrate how old predictions were on the point of fulfilment. The foe from the North could now be identified.' See *ZAW* 67, 1955, 229.

[3] Ezekiel in ch. 26 prophesies that Nebuchadnezzar will capture Tyre, and gives a vivid impression of the catastrophe that this will represent; and in ch. 29 he coolly tells his listeners that, since Nebuchadnezzar was unsuccessful in his siege of Tyre, God will give him the conquest of Egypt instead.

ancient customary law accepted long before Moses could have lived. But the question is not, whether or not a 'Law of Moses' existed, but whether or not the religion was organized upon the basis of the authority of that 'Law'. The evidence of the historical books and the prophets suggests that, even if the Law of Moses existed as it now does, the religion was not in that time explicitly organized around submission to the Law. The structure of religious life in the time of the kings is markedly different from the structure of a scriptural religion.

Our mention of the Law of Moses, however, leads us on to a further point. This argument started without any substantial use of historical analysis, and by just looking at the Bible as it stands. But it is natural to add a historical and critical parameter here. The sort of evidence I have briefly presented suggests that the broad reaches of critical opinion, best represented by Wellhausen, have been right in judging that the Law of Moses, as represented and understood in the late forms of the Pentateuch and in late documents like Ezra, is the result of a late stage in the development of the Old Testament. It was the Deuteronomic movement, around the eighth and seventh centuries, that began to make something like a 'scripture' central to the life of Israel. It was with it and with Josiah and his scroll found in the temple that something like a definite *book* comes into the centre of the religious life of the nation. It is here that one hears that the words of this 'book' are to be pored over and pondered at all times and that nothing is to be added to it or taken away from it (Deut. 4:2), the phrase that most clearly formulates what was eventually to become the principle of the *canon*. It is likely that much of the present organization of materials within the Pentateuch as Mosaic law came after the establishment of this principle. This does not mean necessarily that all the material, as material, is of late date, and critical scholars have not generally supposed so; what is likely to be of late date is the *recognition* that this material, seen as Mosaic law, is of paramount authority and beyond comparison with any other source or instance. My argument in what follows does not depend upon this critical construction but it gains from it and I think it is highly probable. Thus, to sum up again: if we are to imagine and enter into the life of Israel in its older times, we have to enter into the experience of men who had no scripture in a sense comparable with what Christians have long understood themselves to have.

This does not mean, indeed, that of the Old Testament as we now have it just nothing existed. Considerable strata of that which we now read as our Old Testament were already in existence, and were developing. These included the authoritative national-religious traditions, and these would in due course become more fixed in form, be written down, and achieve the status of what later came to be called 'scripture'. But, central and authoritative as these traditions were, they still differed in many ways from the later idea of 'scripture'. They were still in process of change, growth, and development. They were not intrinsically separable from the general life of all the traditions of the community. Above all, there was not, as there is with our Bible, a permanent, unchanging, qualitative line of demarcation, objectively indicating what is within and what is without. One may look at a Bible and say that, as an objective fact, at least for the normal English Bible, the Book of Daniel is within and the Book of Enoch is not within; but in ancient Israel there was no such objectively visible line to separate between the accepted and authoritative traditions and other traditions that circulated in the community.

If in the earlier stages, however, the religion of Old Testament is not yet a scriptural religion, in the later stages we see it becoming exactly that. In Deuteronomy, as already stated, we perhaps first find the use of the term 'book' as a comprehensive and complete 'scripture', a written holy book containing the essential requirements for the obedience of Israel to God.[4] It is probably only in late times that we begin to find within the Old Testament itself actual references back, integral to the text and not mere glosses, literary similarities or allusions, but explicit references to a pre-existing book as a source requiring to be explained or interpreted. Thus in the late book of Daniel, generally assigned to the Maccabaean period, second century BC, we find: 'I, Daniel, perceived *in the*

---

[4] The Hebrew word *sepher*, which we often think of as 'book', in ancient times often meant something more like a 'document'—a paper, account or contract, such as a woman's divorce document (Deut. 24:1), and not a book in our sense.

books the number of years which, according to the word of
the Lord to Jeremiah the prophet, must pass before the end of
the desolations of Jerusalem, namely, seventy years' (Dan.
9:2, referring to Jer. 29:10). Here we have a man really
worrying about the interpretation of pre-existing scripture:
what can it mean when it says in the book of Jeremiah that
seventy years will see the end of the desolations of Jerusalem?
And so the angel explains to him the meaning of the
prophecy: it means not seventy years, but seventy weeks of
years. And so Daniel can draw the conclusions for his own
time.[5]

This does not mean that there is not a great deal of cross-
reference between one Old Testament source and another.
The material was national literature and there were a
multitude of cross-references to things known from another
source, or known generally in the culture and independently
used by more than one source. For instance, the command to
keep the Sabbath in the Exodus form of the Ten Command-
ments (Exod. 20:11) made reference to the creation of the
world in seven days, a clear cross-reference to the first chapter
of Genesis. Nevertheless the extent of such cross-reference
should not be exaggerated. The evidence suggests a rather
loose relation between books and traditions, not the tightly
defined network of relations implied when an exactly
demarcated 'scripture' has come into existence. The cross-
reference to creation at this point was not essential to the
expression of the Sabbath commandment, as is shown by the
fact that the formulation of the same commandment in
Deuteronomy does not make this reference to creation at all,
but provides a quite different 'motivation' for the same
command (Deut. 5:14f.). When Ecclesiastes speaks of how
'the dust returns to the earth as it was, and the spirit returns to
God who gave it' (12:7), this undoubtedly draws upon the
same world of ideas and images as Gen. 2–3, but it is unlikely
that it should count as a cross-reference to another 'scripture'.

It was, then, only late in the development of the Old

---

[5] Similarly in the New Testament it is in the latest documents that one finds the first
explicit mention of the other documents and the problems occasioned by their
interpretation: 2 Pet. 3:15f. on the Pauline letters.

Testament that its faith began to turn into a scriptural religion, and this change meant a fateful and all-important change in the character of the religion. In the last centuries before the coming of Christianity, Judaism became a scriptural religion in a sense in which its preceding stages had never been one. There was now a clearly-defined holy written document, the Torah, which in its entirety had come from God and which had near-absolute authority in religion and morality. There were also other books of profoundly authoritative religious status—in effect, much of the rest of what we now call the Old Testament—but the question of its definition and clarity must be left to a later point.[6] It was in essence the clear definition of the Torah as supreme holy book that created the scriptural character of Judaism.

With this we pass to the New Testament and its relations to the Old. By this time Judaism was already, and had long been, what I have called a scriptural religion, and its collection of holy books, roughly what we now call the Old Testament,[7] was of central importance. The recognition of the Torah as supreme was widespread if not universal.[8] The scripturality of Judaism by this time is not only a historical fact, but a matter of profound theological significance. Jesus came into a world where there was already a scripture. One must, however, use discrimination in evaluating the significance of this and the biblical statements about it. This relationship between Jesus and the Old Testament scriptures has been of the utmost importance in the history of doctrine, because it provided most of the sayings which traditional Christianity, and especially Protestant orthodoxy, used to build up its doctrine of scripture. When Jesus appealed to the Old Testament with the term γέγραπται 'it is written', when he spoke of it as the Word of God, when he said that it could not be 'broken' (John 10:35), when he said that 'not an iota, not a dot' (Matt. 5:18, RSV) would pass away from the law until all should be accomplished, all this referred to the Old Testament. These sayings made no reference to any 'New

---

[6] See below, pp. 49–61.
[7] I say 'roughly' for a reason that will be taken up later; see below, pp. 61f.
[8] Cf. below, pp. 51f.

Testament scriptures' at all. Nevertheless traditional Christianity used all these passages, and others like them, to support its doctrinal picture not of the Old Testament alone but of the entire Christian scripture of Old and New Testaments. It did this because it proceeded from its own starting point of the entire Christian Bible, and assumed that what was true of one part of it would be true of another. It never thought that the relation between scripture and religion, scripture and faith, might be different in one part as against another. Most of all, Protestant orthodoxy in particular read into these evidences its own ideals and convictions of a religion strictly controlled by scripture and subservient to it, and never considered the possibility that the texts might, or even must, be read in another way.

That Jesus came into a world where there was already an authoritative scripture, and a community within which it was interpreted, was immensely important. The Old Testament provided much of the essential conceptuality of the New—not all, but much that was essential. And this was not in the realm of ideas only. It was, one may say, if one follows the Gospels, the existence of scripture that brought Jesus to his clash with the Jewish leaders of his time and thus to his death. The conflict between scripture and the existing Jewish interpretations of it, and the dialectic between it and Jesus' own religious ideas and ideas of himself, brought about the deep and tragic conflicts between Jesus and the leaders of his people, which in turn brought him to rejection and death, and brought mankind to salvation. Thus the Old Testament is not only intellectually essential in providing categories and imagery for the understanding of Jesus Christ, it is also functional in salvation through the chain of events within his ministry and up to his passion. This is a theme that I made central to an earlier book[9] and I still think that it cannot be sufficiently emphasized.

But—and this is a difference that has seldom been properly noticed and evaluated—all this enormous importance of the Old Testament for the New does not mean that the New Testament faith was from the beginning—or indeed within

[9] *Old and New in Interpretation* (London: SCM, 1966).

the main body of the existing New Testament—designed or destined to be a scriptural religion in the way in which by that time the religion grown out of the Old Testament had become a scriptural religion. Therefore, the texts expressing Jesus' attitudes to the Old Testament were by no means equal to, or even particularly relevant for, the task to which they have so often been put, namely that of establishing the status of scripture *within Christianity*.

Jesus in his teaching is nowhere portrayed as commanding or even sanctioning the production of a written Gospel, still less a written New Testament. He never even casually told his disciples to write anything down, nor did he even, short of writing, command them to memorize his words exactly for future committal to the medium of writing. It is possible of course to theorize that writing was, in fact and in the culture, more important than is actually expressed in the Gospels, and that it was tacitly understood that as much as possible must be committed to writing. But this is pure hypothesis, if not pure wishful thinking. There is not a single point at which Jesus commands that an event or a teaching should be written down so that it would be accurately remembered. The probability lies in the opposite direction: that, in spite of the existence of previous scripture in the form of the Old Testament (as we call it now), the cultural presupposition suggested that committal to writing was an *unworthy* mode of transmission of the profoundest truth. On the Greek side Plato had argued exactly this, and the Pharisees seem to have had a strong tradition to the effect that the oral traditions should *not* be written down.[10] Paul's statement that 'the letter killeth, but spirit giveth life' (2 Cor. 3:6 KJV), though not in itself referring to the question whether there should be a written New Testament or not, surely reveals a similar underlying cultural assumption: the idea of the fatal effect of writing was not a novelty. We do not have to press this point, however, too far. We only have to recognize that the idea of a Christian faith governed by Christian written holy scriptures was not an essential part of the foundation plan of Christianity. In due course indeed it turned out to be desirable for

[10] On this see B. Gerhardsson, *Memory and Manuscript* (Uppsala: Gleerup, 1961).

many reasons that the story of Jesus should be written down, and this was in fact done; but there is no reason to believe that this was planned or intended by Jesus himself or, in the early stages, by his followers. Those who have suggested that 'holy scripture' was not a basic or original Christian idea and that the production of the first written Gospel was a failure of nerve or even a manifestation of the persistence of original sin, even if we do not agree with them, were not at all on unreasonable ground—or indeed on unscriptural ground—in so arguing.[11] Far from Christianity, within New Testament times, being dependent on the existence of written Christian scriptures, it was clearly possible for the faith to be spread and communicated in the world without the existence of a connected story of Jesus such as our Gospels, or even their sources, offer. The earliest Christian documents now extant, the early letters of St. Paul, are of course written texts, and this for the obvious reason, that it is of the nature of a letter that it must be written. Though themselves written texts, these letters display no consciousness of the dependence of Christianity upon a basis lying in Christian written scriptures. Thus, to sum up again, it is not at all clear from the New Testament itself that Jesus or the earliest Christians intended Christianity to be a scriptural religion, a faith bound and controlled by its own scriptures and one in which such scriptures would have ultimate authoritative status: indeed, the New Testament seems to make it clear that they did not so intend.

What then of those utterances of Jesus—and Paul and others—about the authority of the Old Testament? Do these not make it clear that the Christian message rested on a scriptural basis and included the authority of scripture—that is, of the Old Testament—among its claims? Yes, of course it was so: *of course* the Old Testament was the Word of God, *of course* it had authority, *of course* it was true that its words would not pass away and could not be broken. All this is true, and what is more, it is absolutely essential: for it is not merely a question of scripture, it goes farther and is a recognition that

---

[11] Cf. C.F. Evans and R.H. Lightfoot as cited in my *The Bible in the Modern World* (London: SCM, 1973), pp. 43f., 128.

the entire revelation of the God of Israel in ancient times is valid and true revelation of the God who is now known as the God and Father of Jesus Christ. But, though this is true and essential, it is not as decisive for the question under discussion as it has seemed to be.

For the undisputed status of the Old Testament as Word of God did not alter the fact that, for the men of the New Testament, the Old Testament, though authoritative, was no longer the communicator of salvation, and in particular not the communicator of salvation to the Gentiles. Only the preaching of Jesus Christ as crucified and risen communicated salvation in the Christian sense. The Old Testament, it was understood, had prophesied that salvation from ancient times, it confirmed and supported the word of that salvation, but it was no longer clear that it in itself was that word. The essential verbal authority was the kerygma of the Gospel, that is, an oral proclamation, more like a sermon than like a Bible. Thus the unquestioned authority of the Old Testament as holy scripture for the early church does not in itself demonstrate that early Christianity had to be supported by a Christian scripture in the same sense in which Judaism, by this time, depended on the Old Testament scripture; and, still more, it does not mean that the New Testament placed itself under the *control* of the Old, as if the Old was its final criterion or the absolute source for the derivation of religious truth. The New Testament itself makes it entirely clear that it was neither of these. The idea of a near-absolute scriptural *control* of faith is a quite foreign conception, based on a quite different construct of problems, and read into the New Testament statements about Old Testament scripture by a later generation, especially in Protestant orthodoxy, for which the concept of scriptural *control* of religion and doctrine was of absolute importance.[12]

As has already been remarked, Jesus' sayings about the continuing and inviolable authority of the Old Testament were constantly exploited in traditional theology, and especially in Protestant orthodoxy, in order to make it seem that

---

[12] On this see in general H. von Campenhausen, *The Formation of the Christian Bible* (London: A. & C. Black, 1972), pp. 1–61.

Christianity was intended to be a strictly scriptural religion, absolutely submitted to its holy book and unquestioning in its obedience to it. But the effect of this argument has commonly been to diminish and depreciate the originality of Jesus and the creativity of his own understanding and thus to assimilate him—against all the evidence of his own teaching—to the pattern of the scribal interpreter. For it is crystal clear that Jesus' stance towards the Old Testament, as depicted in the Gospels, is a critical and independent one. 'It has been said to you by those of ancient time, you shall not kill... but I say unto you...' (Matt. 5:21): the contrast is obvious, and it forms one of the great classic passages of the Sermon on the Mount. Jesus does not derogate from the authority of the Old Testament law: it remains the Word of God, it remains authoritative, it will not pass away, Jesus is come not to abolish it but to fulfil it. But, true as this is, it is not the main point. The main point is that Jesus in his teaching is not bound and controlled by these laws and goes far beyond them; the law does not constitute the basis and authority of his teaching, and the range and power of his teaching is not controlled by the meaning of the laws. Jesus was not merely an interpreter of these laws but one who declared his own teaching on the basis of his own authority. Or we may perhaps put it in this way: Jesus' teaching denies the literal meaning of the law and proclaims a spiritual meaning. But a spiritual meaning is of such a kind, by its own nature, that its content is not determined directly and exclusively by the text being interpreted; a new factor, other than the scriptural text, has gained authority and begun to determine the meaning. The oft-quoted words 'Think not that I have come to abolish the law and the prophets' (Matt. 5:17) are significant and necessary precisely because, as the sequel immediately makes clear, Jesus' teaching is about to range far beyond anything that could be justified as an interpretation of these laws. Even if we use the formulation that Jesus, by the series of contrasts between the laws, himself and his teaching, was 'fulfilling' these laws, the 'fulfilment' is not of such a kind that one could say it is controlled by the actual text of the laws. Thus the Old Testament remains entirely authoritative, but it does not provide or constitute Jesus' teaching about the Kingdom of

God.[13] On the contrary, if for Jesus the authority of the Old
Testament had been absolute, so that nothing could be said
that was not authorized by it, then there would have been no
Christian Gospel. Recent trends have been entirely right in
emphasizing the Jewish roots and setting of the Gospel; but it
is equally true that Christianity is not a mere mild modification of Judaism, or a supplement to the Old Testament, or
even a final interpretation of the latter, but is something
radically new, that goes completely beyond the bounds of
what the Old Testament and/or Judaism had contemplated.

One example of this lies in the idea of incarnation itself. It
may be rightly said that incarnation became possible and
meaningful only on Jewish soil, since the Old Testament
established the deep distinction between the divine and the
human which alone could serve as the wholesome presupposition for incarnation and set it on a basis different from the
mythological mixtures of human and divine known in many
religions. This may well be so, but it is hardly possible to stop
there; for, if the Old Testament did this, it also—at least in its
main theological trends, as apart from occasional survivals,
uses of old mythical imagery, and the like—made combinations of the divine and the human impossible, unthinkable,
and forbidden. For Jesus to say, if he did say it, 'I am the Son
of God' (John 10:36) was surely to transgress some of the
deepest teaching of the Old Testament in its most authoritative strata; and if it is true that Jews took up stones to stone
him 'because you, being a man, make yourself God' (10:33),
they surely had reasonably good scriptural authority for
doing so (Lev. 24:16). The words and deeds of both Jesus and
the Jews may be unhistorical at this point but this makes no
difference: they properly symbolize the consequences of the
idea of incarnation.[14] In fact incarnation is one part of

---

[13] 'By the commands which Jesus proclaims the ancient Torah is not merely
surpassed, but superseded.... As Lord of his people Jesus thrusts aside the limited
commands of the existing law with his mighty "But I say unto you".... In face of
Jesus' superior authority the Law can no longer be invoked as a court of
appeal.... Surprisingly, however, the fact that the Law is thus outstripped means not
that it is abolished but precisely that it is reaffirmed'—so Campenhausen, op. cit., pp.
12–13. I am not sure that I myself would go so far as to say 'superseded' in the first
sentence.

[14] It may well be that Jesus, seen historically, carefully refrained from making claims

Christian belief for which the Old Testament (and, still more, post-biblical Judaism) had furnished little positive preparation. Notice, moreover, that Jesus does not dispute the understanding of the prohibition against blasphemy by these Jews; rather, he refers on the one hand to his own good works, and on the other he quotes the 'You are gods' of Ps. 82:6 so as to suggest that it is possible for those to whom the Word of God has come to be called 'gods'. But this passage, as the Jews would have been quick to see, was no kind of demonstration of the reality of incarnation, nor was it a diminution of the force of the charge of blasphemy. It is Jesus' own self and mission, and his good works, that provide the force for his argument and put material strength into the scripture quoted by him. It is not surprising that the church tradition, in working out the implications of incarnation, had to turn in some measure to the use of non-Hebraic concepts.

A second example lies in the ethical teaching of Jesus. The ethical judgement and ethos of many parts of the Old Testament contains a strong eudaemonistic element, if we may so call it, a stress on the family and its cohesion, and on the wealth and prosperity with which great men like Abraham and Job are rewarded. In Jesus' teaching these considerations are greatly minimized. The family is a threat to one's obedience to God, one has to be ready to drop one's obligations to it, rewards are not to be expected in this world, riches are a danger and a temptation, and the obedient must expect suffering, persecution and loss. Jesus may or may not be original in all this; there are of course some precedents in rabbinic and sectarian Judaism and in other sources of his time. And even within the Old Testament there are certain sources and passages which go somewhat in the same direction. But it seems simply impossible to suppose that in his basic ethical values Jesus is following the guidance of the main currents of the Old Testament.

---

of divinity for himself, as is vividly seen in the Synoptic Gospels. The case indicates one of the dilemmas of the traditional conservative appeal to John, where the 'claim' of Jesus to be God is supposed to be validated. But that same 'claim', if it was actually expressed, would strongly refute that other conservative idea, namely that Jesus fulfilled the Old Testament but never went beyond it or contradicted it in any way.

A third example will be mentioned only briefly here, because we shall return to it later.[15] I refer to the prominence of the *parable* as genre for the teaching of Jesus. The parable, generally speaking, is not interpretation of pre-existing scripture and does not take such scripture as its starting point: its basis lies in something entirely different.

All these examples show how, in spite of the continued authority accorded to the Old Testament within Christianity, the Old Testament was by no means its controlling and delimiting authority. With Jesus there came something new, something that burst the limits of what the Old Testament knew about; and for the expression of that something new it was both necessary and right that Jesus' teaching should go far beyond what scripture then authorized and should also be, whether openly or implicitly, critical in its attitude to scripture. The authority attached to the Old Testament within the New did not mean that New Testament Christianity took pre-existing scripture as its dominant and controlling ideological base. To read the New Testament references to the authority of the Old as if they meant this is to read them in a way that quite contradicts the New Testament situation.

The people of the time, as the Gospels depict them, recognized a difference here: 'this man is not like the scribes, for he teaches with authority'. Now the scribes had behind them the authority of tradition, but they also had behind them the authority of scripture;[16] what they did not have was authority of their own. Jesus was not limited to the methods and techniques of scribal interpretation: he was able to *declare* on the basis of his own authority what the meaning of scripture was and, if necessary, to state the truth on his own authority whether there was scripture for it or not. When traditional (and especially Protestant) Christianity took the remarks of Jesus about the authority of the Jewish scriptures and used them as building blocks for the construction of a

---

[15] See below, p. 69.
[16] It is unworthy denigration of the scribes to suggest that they based their thinking merely on 'human' traditions and not also, or even more, on scripture; scripture, after all, is exactly what they were scribes of. Once again I must add: Jesus may have been historically much closer to the methods of Jewish scribes than the Gospels suggest; but my argument is based on the situation as the Gospels depict it.

picture of a Christianity which would equally be a completely scriptural religion, they were to that extent assimilating the Christian faith to the pattern of Judaism and reducing its difference and originality. The undoubted authority of the Old Testament as Word of God does not alter the fact that for the New Testament it is no longer the unique starting point: its positions may be criticized, may be modified, and it is no longer an absolute. Its authority is relative to the supreme authority of Jesus Christ. In this respect New Testament Christianity, as it was within the time of the growth of the New Testament itself, was not really a scriptural religion, a religion of the Book. It did not really have, at its basis, its own Bible—yet.

This may be confirmed when we consider the rather limited attention given in the New Testament to what would now be called the 'doctrine of scripture': indeed it might not be going too far to say that the New Testament is not interested in the 'doctrine of scripture' at all. Stern warnings of Jesus attach to ethical matters: the day of judgement will be a bad time for certain cities because of their receipt of him, for certain persons because they have failed to tend the poor and needy; but there is no suggestion that man on the day of judgement will be questioned about what doctrine of scripture he has held.[17] New Testament religion, especially in the formative earlier decades, is not much concerned by such questions. There are warnings about false prophets (e.g. Matt. 7:15ff.) but no suggestion that scripture will enable us to know which prophets are false and which are not: on the contrary, it is by their fruits, by the ethical consequences of their personality

[17] It may not at first sight be obvious why this example should be relevant. Did anyone ever say that the doctrine of scripture would be a matter of questioning on the day of judgement? Probably not. Nevertheless it is implied, and in a way very important for the understanding of sectarianism. Separation from other Christians is an extremely serious matter, forbidden in principle by the faith. Separation cannot be justified just because we do not agree with others: it must imply that God himself is believed to condemn or reject them. Seen from this point of view, the comparison with the sayings about the day of judgement is very relevant. There is no evidence that God condemns anyone for their doctrine of scripture. Therefore the doctrine of scripture can never be a reason for separation from fellowship. This means that much sectarianism, taking the doctrine of scripture as its criterion, has been contrary to scripture in this respect. Difference over the doctrine of scripture is never a reason for supposing that other believers are not in full and true communion with God.

and teaching, that they are to be known. When St. John tells us (2 John 9–10), in words that were to become the foundation charter of Protestant sectarianism, that one must separate from all those who do not have the true doctrine of Christ, not greeting them nor welcoming them into one's house, he gives no indication that scripture will be the criterion of the truth in question. In fact scripture is never mentioned in the three Johannine letters, although Cain is cited as a negative example (1 John 3:12). In the New Testament scripture is used again and again as demonstration, as confirmatory evidence, as argumentative material, but there is no evidence that it was thought of, or could be thought of, as the ultimate criterion of Christian truth. It is not surprising, therefore, that St. Paul was able to write central theological letters like Galatians and Romans without spending much time on the nature of biblical authority.

It was, characteristically, in the later margin of the New Testament that assertions more precisely directed towards the character of scripture came to be developed. But even here the concentration of attention on scripture falls far short of what was later, on the basis of the completed Bible, conceived. The famous passage 2 Tim. 3:16, the traditional key passage for the idea of inspiration, reads: 'All scripture is inspired by God and profitable for teaching, for reproof, for correction, and for training in righteousness, that the man of God may be complete, equipped for every good work' (RSV). Here indeed we have an assertion of biblical inspiration, and one of the most overworked texts in the entire Bible, comparable in this respect only with Matt. 16:18 'You are Peter, and on this rock I will build my church'. The striking thing about 2 Tim. 3:16 is not its declaration of scriptural inspiration but its unstressed and low-key application of it. It is not remarkable that it says nothing about inerrancy or historical accuracy, which were not an issue at the time or until many centuries later; but, more important, it says nothing about scripture being the foundation of the Christian faith, or the ultimate criterion of its genuineness, or the decisive factor above all others in the understanding of it. What it does say is that scripture is *useful, profitable*, for the needs of the pastoral ministry. The verse belongs to practical rather than to dogmatic theology. The study of scripture, because scripture is inspired by God, is immensely profitable for training in the Christian life, for sanctification, improvement and equipment. This is the burden also of the previous verse: since childhood Timothy has known 'sacred letters', ἱερὰ γράμματα, which will have been 'able' (δυνάμενα) to instruct him in salvation through faith in Christ Jesus. For the writer of 2 Timothy there is a body of inspired scripture, not clearly defined so far as we can tell, which was enormously useful for the needs of the Christian life;[18] but there is no hint that there was an inspired and defined 'Bible' which was the source from which Christian truth must be derived and the touchstone by which it must in all regards be tested. The familiar understanding of the passage, which takes it as the prime source for the doctrine of complete scriptural control of Christianity, is one reached through reading into 2 Timothy, or more correctly into this one sentence, the questions and situations of a later age.

In all these ways the world within the Bible is very different from the world as perceived when the Bible, already formed and demarcated, is taken as a unitary body of material uniquely authoritative as controlling criterion for faith. When traditional Christianity took its doctrinal starting point, for this sort of question, with the *completed* scripture, assuming the delimitation of it through the canon, it produced a picture which, though greatly emphasizing the authority of the Bible, was considerably at variance with the situation as known to the men of the Bible themselves, the situation therefore that underlay their own statements and thus formed their semantic content. Where this is so, the effect is not that biblical statements are denied, but that their meaning is misread.

The effect of this is to point to a great paradox: simply to *magnify* the authority of the Bible is not to improve in any way the chance that it is understood. In many traditions of Christianity the *principle* of the authority of scripture has been magnified as far as it can be done, but this runs into the

---

[18] The question whether the passage means 'all scripture is inspired ... and profitable' or 'all inspired scripture is profitable' does not seem in itself to make much difference to the matter under discussion.

ultimate difficulty that, when one enters into the Bible itself one finds that its own actual statements, taken as they stand, indicate a rather more relative and less absolute emphasis. The question then is, whether the phenomena of the biblical texts themselves are to be allowed to revise and remake our principles, or whether our principles are to be read into the biblical texts, even at the cost of obscuring their meaning. These two approaches may be usefully distinguished as the deductive and the inductive approaches to the nature of the Bible.[19] The deductive approach may begin from such considerations as the following: is it not necessary that Christian faith should have an accessible and articulate authority? if there is such an authority, is it not necessary that it should be divinely given and constructed, in such a way that human tampering cannot have affected it? if it is so divinely given, does it not necessarily follow that it is free from any kind of error? The inductive approach will begin from a quite different set of observations: is it not the case that the Bible itself contains only rather limited assertions about the existence and function of scripture within Christianity? did not the men of the New Testament live by personal contact and oral tradition rather than by submission to a written document? does not the Bible itself contain very various estimates of the place, role, and authority of different parts of itself? does it not contain pseudonymous documents and the like? The importance of the difference between these two approaches will be continuously before us in the following discussions.

[19] The terms are so used in W.J. Abraham, *The Divine Inspiration of Holy Scripture* (Oxford: Clarendon Press, 1981), titles of chapters 1 and 2.

II

Biblical authority and biblical criticism in the conflict of church traditions

THE distinction established in the first chapter between the situation where the Bible already stood complete as an acknowledged and delimited canon and the situation of the men of the Bible themselves, who in many respects did not have any such complete 'scripture', has now received a preliminary discussion in respect of the biblical evidence itself. But before we go farther we should provide another preliminary discussion, which will concern primarily the outworking of these problems in the more modern theological tradition, especially from the Reformation to the present day.

We may start once again with Protestant orthodoxy, for which the doctrine of scripture was of absolutely paramount importance: the Westminster Confession, a good example, placed its formulation of this doctrine right at the beginning, before any other matters at all were considered. Scripture was given by inspiration of God, and the scope of its operation was defined with extreme precision: all the sixty-six books of the (Protestant) canon were completely inspired; no other books were inspired at all; everything else, however good, belonged at the best to human tradition or ecclesiastical opinion. Verbal inspiration meant that all the words of the text of exactly these books were inspired and therefore infallible. All doctrinal formulation was to be strictly guided and controlled by scripture and by no other comparable source of authority: the physical manifestation of this is provided by the mass of proof-texts attached as footnotes to the Confession.

One of the difficulties about this lies, however, in the question of the canon itself. It was impossible to provide *scriptural* proof for this most central of questions, namely, which precisely were the books which had been divinely inspired. No passage in either Old or New Testament gave a list, nor indeed, as we shall shortly see, did any passage give any indication that they cared seriously about the question. The List of Contents prefaced to the Bible, though it was all-important for the total shape of what lay within, was not part of the inspired text of the Bible itself. For *evidence* about what was within the canon, one had to go outside the canon itself. The most ancient precise evidence that could have supported the (Protestant) idea of the Old Testament canon lay, paradoxically, in Josephus, hardly an inspired source by Reformational criteria;[1] or, if not in Josephus, then in Fourth Ezra, which tells (4 Ezra 14:37ff.) how, after the Law had been burned and lost, and must be restored, five men under the direction of Ezra wrote what had been dictated in order, producing ninety-four books. Afterwards the Most High spoke to Ezra saying that the twenty-four should be made public so that all should read in them, but the other seventy should be kept and delivered only to the wise. This is a text that is really interested in the numbering and delimiting of the books, and at least some people, one supposes, have thought it to be an inspired work: it is part of the Latin Bible, even if only in an appendix nowadays. But of course it was no more possible to use 4 Ezra than to use Josephus as proof of a Protestant orthodox view of scripture: 4 Ezra was a book itself considered apocryphal, and—even worse—it expressly sanctioned the authority of no less than seventy additional works, outside the accepted Jewish canon.

But, these exotic sources being ruled out, there was, on the

---

[1] In fact certain secondary versions of parts of Josephus' works did succeed in gaining a kind of canonical status in certain churches: notably the so-called *Zena 'ayhud*, part of the normal Ethiopic Bible; and cf. also the place of the Slavonic Josephus in the older Russian culture. The appeal of these works, however, lay in the history of the Jews rather than in Josephus' views about the canon. His passage (c. Ap. i. 37–41) does not give the actual names of the books: there are five books of Moses, thirteen books written by prophets to continue the history after Moses, and four books containing 'hymns to God and precepts for the conduct of human life'. If one takes together certain books, e.g. Judges and Ruth, Jeremiah and Lamentations, this enumeration can fit that of the present Jewish (and Protestant) canons. The number twenty-two has often been associated with that of the number of letters in the Hebrew alphabet. The twenty-four books of 4 Ezra do not imply a different total scripture, only a different way of reckoning. Josephus' reckoning, though compatible with the Jewish and Protestant numbers for the canon as a whole, does not agree with the now traditional Jewish grouping into three stages of Law, Prophets, and Writings; on this see below, p. 55, and cf. Appendix I, pp. 127ff., for some of the relevant texts.

orthodox view, no *scriptural* evidence to decide what were the exact limits of the canon. Books do not necessarily say whether they are divinely inspired or not, and many books that do in some fashion claim divine inspiration were nevertheless not accepted as canonical. It is impossible to know exactly which books were supposed by the author to be included in the πᾶσα γραφή of 2 Tim. 3:16. On the grounds that, in this late New Testament period, the Pauline letters were already by implication classed as γραφαί (2 Pet. 3:16), we may consider it likely that some New Testament writings, as well as those of the Old, were intended. But, on the same ground, a work like Enoch, apparently familiar to the writer of Jude (Jude 14) and cited by him as having been 'prophesied' verbatim by Enoch, is also likely to have been among the ἱερὰ γράμματα 'sacred letters' (without article!) on which Timothy had been brought up. It is on the whole rather likely that the letter to Timothy was based on a recognition of some writings that later counted as apocryphal and a non-recognition of some that later counted as canonical. It is even more likely that the letter, in spite of its fine words about 'inspired' scripture, had no idea that this implied a strict definition of certain limited sets of writings as inspired, with the necessary consequence that all other writings were non-inspired.

On a flexible view of inspiration this would not matter much. But where, as in Protestant orthodoxy, the frontiers of inspiration were regarded as clear-cut and as of absolute qualitative importance, the consequence of this, if it had been faced, would have been appalling. for it would have meant that doctrine was being derived from non-inspired books, and, even worse, that this or that inspired book was being wrongly classified and left out of the reckoning in the construction of doctrine. But this problem was not seen, because the results of the various decisions about the canon made in Protestantism, some of them going back to Judaism and to the earlier church, were simply read into any biblical texts that said something about 'scripture'. Perhaps the matter was viewed in a purely supernaturalistic way: God had in fact inspired exactly the sixty-six books of the Protestant canon, and when the word 'scripture' was used in places like 2

Timothy or 2 Peter he meant it to mean exactly that set of books. In itself this is logically quite coherent; but even on these terms it is still mere supposition: there was and could be no *scriptural proof* that the sixty-six books were the uniquely inspired set of books. The precise boundary of the canon was not known from scripture, but was assumed.

Appeal could be made to the Fathers and to tradition but, as the Reformers well knew, the Fathers and tradition were disunited over exactly this matter. Protestantism in following the Hebrew canon for the most part agreed with the judgement of Jerome; but Augustine, who in point of actual theological content was a far more powerful authority for Protestant doctrine, was in this quite against Jerome's opinion.[2] In fact few people in the older Protestantism troubled about the question. To them, on the whole, the canon seemed to be self-evidenced: what was in the Bible was, manifestly, the inspired set of books. This way of stating the matter, however, is surely no more than a gigantic fiction, covering over the fact that the word 'scripture' was now being defined in a sense possibly quite at variance with the meaning of the biblical passages in which it occurred.[3] It was not surprising, therefore, that one of the vital stages in the development of modern biblical research, with Semler, concerned in particular the canon.[4]

A second and related matter was the status of tradition. As Protestant orthodoxy saw it, tradition was a human affair, which might be better or be worse, but was absolutely different in character from inspired scripture. Tradition had come from men, but scripture came from God; the distinction in this form, used by Protestants against the Roman Catholic position, was built upon the terms of the controversy in the Gospels between Jesus and the scribes and Pharisees. Thus many Protestants found it difficult to admit that scripture was a product of the community, just as they found it difficult to admit that the church had established the canon. They

---

[2] Cf. H.F.D. Sparks in the *Cambridge History of the Bible*, i. 534.
[3] For thoughts in this area, along with useful quotations from classic sources, cf. K. Barth, *KD* I/2, 524ff., 666ff.; E.T., *CD* I/2, 473ff., 597ff.
[4] On this cf. G. Hornig, *Die Anfänge der historisch-kritischen Theologie* (Göttingen, 1961).

thought rather that in the order of revelation scripture was antecedent to the church: the church came into being, as it were, when it heard rightly the voice of scripture, which was there before it. And this was indeed a possible way of thinking, if one took one's starting-point with the new generations of the church, after the Bible and its canon were already complete. For each new generation of the church the Bible is already there beforehand, in response to its message faith is generated and thereby the true life of the church goes forward. It is the completed document scripture that presents itself to each generation; obviously therefore everything depends on the status of this document. If one sees things in this way, it becomes natural to see the *writing*, the creation of the complete written document, as the key locus of the special communication which comes to bear upon the church. It was *the writers* who were guided by God and protected from error.

Today, however, we recognize that the production of scripture was preceded by a period of tradition, long in some cases, shorter in others. Some of the earlier stages were earlier written sources or documents, which were used in the final editing of the books as we know them. Other earlier stages were oral, and this may have meant that the 'text' existed in a fairly fluid state. We do not have to determine the proportions between these two. In either case the stages before the final production of the book as it now stands may have been, indeed must have been, much the more creative and productive. In these circumstances it becomes impossibly artificial to attribute divine inspiration particularly to the writing of the texts in their final form. If there is inspiration at all, then it must extend over the entire process of production that has led to the final text. Inspiration therefore must attach not to a small number of exceptional persons like St. Matthew or St. Paul: it must extend over a large number of anonymous persons, so much so that it must be considered to belong more to the community as a whole than to a group of quite exceptional persons who through unique inspiration 'gave' the scriptures to the community. In this sense scripture emerged from the community: it was a product of the church.

This does not mean that we can ignore the traditional conception that 'the church is born from the Word of God'.

There is not only tradition, but also an input into the tradition. The Bible was not just the result of a development of thought on the basis of earlier tradition; it derived also from the input of radically new materials. This input can be described, perhaps, as the kerygma or the Gospel: the teaching of John the Baptist, the teaching of Jesus, the new events which marked him out as extraordinary. If the church was born from the Word of God, it was in response to this input. For the earliest church the 'Word of God' was exactly this input: it was not the Bible, nor the New Testament, which had not yet come into existence. The New Testament was the product of the tradition which was generated by this new input. For later generations this input lay embedded within the total material of the Bible. For these later generations it is not surprising that one, speaking inexactly, should speak of the church being born from the hearing of the Word of God, and taking this as if it *was* the Bible, or the New Testament. But within the world of the New Testament itself this was not possible. Once again therefore formulations, which were reasonably natural for the church after the formation and completion of the Bible, were inaccurate if they were applied to the men of the Bible itself, and to their faith.

The Bible, then, is the product of tradition, editing, and revision on the part of the community. But this means that the argument traditionally considered to be 'Catholic', namely that the Bible derived from the church, is in many ways generally valid as against the position esteemed as 'Protestant', which was reluctant to see the Bible as deriving from the church and which therefore sought to give the scripture priority over the church in the order of revelation. The 'Catholic' argument has at least as much justification as the 'Protestant' one.[5] This Protestant view was basically an anachronism: its account of scripture was predicated upon the completed Bible, and upon the distinction between scripture and tradition which was effected by the process of canonization; but it did not provide an account of scripture *as seen*

---

[5] I here qualify the more extreme position I took in my *Explorations in Theology 7* (London: SCM, 1980), p. 116, where I say that the 'Catholic' argument is 'entirely valid'.

from within biblical times, as seen from within the making of
the Bible.

We might perhaps put it in this way: the 'Catholic' position
is the more correct if we ask the question, from where did
scripture come?—but the 'Protestant' understanding may still
be the more correct if we look in the other direction and ask,
to where is scripture directed? For it is certainly not sufficient
to think of scripture as a mere aimless or undirected output of
church tradition: it was directed *to* the community, aimed at
its needs, and had a *normative* relationship to other tradition.
Other tradition, becoming exegetical and thus dependent,
rather than free and independent, accepted this normative
status of scripture. Protestantism was right to observe that
Catholic traditions as they grew had failed to provide
adequate safeguards against the possibility that the interpretative tradition might come to dominate the scripture and
would thus distort its own meaning. Thus both positions in
their way may be both right and in the wrong. It was,
however, the 'Protestant' position that produced the more
serious conflicts and was—at least in the light of hind-
sight—the more obviously contradictory of the factual
character of scripture. Firstly, it laid a much greater stress
upon scripture, and treated it as unique to a degree that set it
apart from any other factor; secondly, its account of scripture
was strongly predicated upon the *origin* of scripture, which
was just the aspect it had got most wrong. Thus when biblical
criticism pointed to evidence that demanded an adjustment of
the traditional views of the nature of scripture, this could
be done only at the cost of risking the shattering of the
entire fabric of Protestant doctrine, or at least of seeming to
do so.

There are, however, many paradoxical turns in these
matters. Roman Catholicism emphasized tradition, and
against the single-minded emphasis on scripture in popular
Protestantism it insisted that scripture came from the church.
But within its own internal thinking it was very slow to take
advantage of this. Around the end of last century and the
beginning of this the Roman church authorities, faced with
biblical criticism and the modernist movement, took refuge in
a conservatism of a type very similar to that made familiar at

about the same time by Protestant fundamentalism. Thus the Gospel of John was written by the original John, Son of Zebedee, who had been the original eye-witness, and it was not permitted to interpret it as if the Gospel had emerged from a stream of 'Johannine' tradition somehow, but more vaguely, related to that John; and similarly with Matthew, with Isaiah, and with Moses. In this way Roman biblical scholars were being prevented from using the dynamics of tradition, which their church understood so well and upon which it built so much, as the model for the understanding of scripture. Only in more recent years, and especially since Vatican II, have Roman Catholic scripture specialists had adequate freedom to interpret scripture in terms of its inner dynamics of tradition, and similarly to interpret it in terms of the literary imagery rather than taking it as strictly dogmatic utterance.

It was actually in Protestantism, or more correctly in the tradition of critical scholarship which had its origins in Protestantism, that the modern emphasis on tradition as the basis for the understanding of scripture was built up. Not that critical scholarship began so much with ideas of tradition. It tended to start out more with ideas concentrating, like orthodoxy, on the individual writer, but to look for the inspiration of genius where orthodoxy had looked for divine dictation. But in the course of the last hundred years it came to emphasize tradition more and more. Contrary to the supposition that biblical criticism isolated and objectivized the 'original' meaning but neglected the dimension of tradition, it was the critical approach which recovered the latter as a dimension *within* scripture as an effective interpretative force; and but for biblical criticism Protestantism would never have come to acknowledge the positive importance of tradition as it has come to do. And, on the other side, the great revival of biblical emphasis in the Roman Catholic church, and all the other changes that have gone along with it, would surely not have happened but for the awareness of modern biblical research. Though the origins of the latter lay for the most part rather on the Protestant side, it could not be identified as a merely Protestant phenomenon: whatever its origins, critical research into the Bible could not be identified with any one religious or theological point of view, and precisely from that point of view it was ecumenically creative.

But this leads on to another paradox. In spite of what has been said about the positive importance of tradition, and the way in which scripture emerged from tradition, we do not suggest that Protestantism was wrong in claiming scripture as its authority and in denying that tradition (after scripture) could be placed on the same level as scripture or that tradition should be allowed to decide what was the right exegesis of scripture. In all this Protestantism was in many ways right. But Protestantism is not proof against the vices which it itself set out to reform. It is perfectly possible today to reiterate the positions of the older Protestant orthodoxy, to regard its judgements as virtually final and to resist the possibility that they might be substantially modified as a result of more modern research into scripture. What then happens is that the traditional 'Catholic' and 'Protestant' roles come to be reversed: the facts of scripture are once again obscured through the imposition of a tradition, but this time it is not a medieval Catholic tradition, it is a Protestant tradition, built upon the insights of the seventeenth century and anxious to maintain these insights *against* the evidence of the text of scripture or at least against the fact that quite different interpretations of the text are possible. When one looks at the various 'conservative', 'orthodox', or 'evangelical' schemes of doctrine which are so influential today, and all of which energetically proclaim the authority of scripture as their first principle, it requires no great insight to see that in many cases it is 'conservatism', or 'Calvinism', or 'evangelicalism' that is the actual authority, and that the authority of the Bible is used and maintained simply because it is supposed to provide the necessary support for the doctrinal authority, which is the real dominant power. The Bible is fully authoritative, but it does not have authority to question the accepted doctrinal tradition. This is analogous to the late medieval position against which the Reformers protested.

Biblical authority on Protestant terms (on Catholic or Orthodox terms it may be otherwise) exists only where one is free, on the ground of scripture, to question, to adjust, and if necessary to abandon the prevailing doctrinal traditions.

Where this freedom does not exist, however much the Bible is celebrated, its authority is in fact submitted to the power of a tradition of doctrine and interpretation. The Protestant approach to scripture can operate only if the actual datum of the biblical text, the *Wortlaut* to use the German term, the actual linguistic and grammatical datum of the text, its form with the semantic implications of that form, can in principle assert itself as against what is alleged to be the interpretation. Hermeneutical methods and principles may be necessary and salutary, but it must be possible to appeal to the text against the dictates of the hermeneutical method. If this is not so, then there is no use in speaking of scriptural authority, because the ultimate authority must attach to the hermeneutical principle. If the Bible says a certain thing, but says it only when understood through an existentialist interpretation, or through a Calvinist interpretation, then it becomes very doubtful whether the Protestant appeal to scripture can be maintained at all. That is to say, the logic of Protestantism must call for freedom in the interpretation of the Bible. The only consistent evangelical position must be that one is willing to listen to, and to take seriously, *any* interpretation of the Bible that seriously professes to be an interpretation of its text, and to judge it through its relation to the biblical text, even if its hermeneutical principles are different from those that have hitherto been accepted.

Freedom and variety in biblical interpretation—these themes carry us on to another major aspect in the relations of Protestantism to the Bible. In the history of ideas great importance attaches to the inability of Protestants to secure agreement among themselves. They had agreement in their opposition to Rome and in their appeal to scripture as the primary authority; but history showed that these were not sufficient to produce doctrinal agreement or ecclesiastical unity and peace. The Protestant insistence that doctrine must be compatible with scripture—and, especially, the specifically Calvinist insistence that doctrine must be not only *compatible* with scripture (as many Lutheran and Anglican reformers held) but must be positively *demonstrable* from scripture— only led to the demonstration—not so surprising after the fact—that scripture, if taken for what it actually said, could support a surprising variety of theological and ecclesiastical positions. If Calvinists found their position clearly proved by scripture, so did Lutherans and so—even more serious—did Arminians; there were Remonstrants in the Netherlands, Socinians in Poland, free-thinkers of all kinds in England, many of them soon to move to the American colonies. All of these groups held scripture to be authoritative. Was their disagreement a proof that the scriptural principle of Protestantism was unworkable?

Protestant sectarianism has been of immense historical importance. It has often been supposed in modern times that biblical criticism was something of essentially German character; but it would be more true to say that it arose in the English-speaking lands, travelled from there to Germany, and eventually returned from Germany to both Britain and America. It is more in the currents of English-speaking thought, free-thinking on the one side, enthusiastic and sectarian on the other, that the origins of biblical criticism lay. It was from these same currents, we may add, that there arose the ideologies that underlay the American Revolution. In sectarian Christianity there was a quite exclusive emphasis on the Bible: confessions, creeds, ministries, church authorities and the like were regarded as largely or purely human quantities, while the Bible came from God. In such groups the struggle for political freedom was also a struggle for freedom to interpret the Bible in ways that differed from those authorized by the prevailing establishment. The question of religious toleration on the social level corresponded with the question of exegetical freedom in the understanding of the Bible.[6]

The concept of freedom is of central importance here, for I wish to suggest that freedom is the central content of the idea of criticism when it is applied to the Bible. Criticism, as I shall later argue, is not one method, such as historical method, nor even a group of methods; it has generated various methods, but it is not in itself a method. In biblical research one can use 'modern methods' or even 'critical methods', without being in

---

[6] On this see the recent major work of H. Reventlow, *Bibelautorität und Geist der Moderne* (Göttingen, 1980).

the least touched by the spirit of criticism; criticism means the freedom, not simply to *use* methods, but to follow them wherever they may lead. Applied to theological problems, this means: the freedom to come to exegetical results which may differ from, or even contradict, the accepted theological interpretation. Criticism in this sense is of course a child of the Enlightenment; but, if so, it is also a child of the Reformation, for the Reformation was expressly 'critical' in this sense.

Freedom is crucial to the understanding of biblical criticism in relation to the churches. The dominant modern conception of freedom comes from the Enlightenment and tends towards secularism. According to it, freedom belongs to the inalienable rights of man and must be protected by an appropriate legal system, which will balance it against the rights and the freedoms of others. Freedom in this sense is an enormous achievement and is not to be underestimated. It is a mistake however to suppose that this constitutes Christian freedom. What is, after all, the basis of Christian freedom? Christian freedom, and the ideas associated with it, primary among them the idea of religious toleration, have commonly been supported upon the basis of the idea of the conscience. Man must have freedom of conscience. It is wrong to force anyone to act against his conscience. The Protestant tradition has expressed itself again and again in these terms. In doing so, however, it was abandoning secure biblical ground. There is nothing in the Bible that supports the enormously inflated role that conscience came to play in the Christianity of the eighteenth and nineteenth centuries. On the one hand the conscience was a sort of divine voice speaking within, a moral guide programmed to lead in the direction willed by God; on the other hand the conscience was a castle of inviolable individual conviction, against which other persons might rage in vain: they might ill-treat the individual, but once they came up against the conscience there was no more that they could do. The view of freedom based upon the conscience was valid, but negative. It rightly recognized that the conscience could not and should not be forced, that there was freedom of conscience. But it left it to the individual conscience to fill itself with the content which would matter. Only if the individual conscience resisted was freedom the best thing. It did not provide a positive reason, *why* man should be free, why it was *better* to have freedom.[7]

The positive ground for Christian freedom lies elsewhere and was best stated by the Lutheran Reformation: the freedom of the Christian man derives from the Gospel and is dependent on justification by faith alone. The believer is fully and freely justified through faith in Christ, and therefore he has no additional religious duties which he must fulfil, in order to carry out his vocation as a Christian. But does this not apply to the biblical scholar? Is it not the vocation of the biblical scholar as believing Christian to carry out the critical examination of scripture?—and, because it is his freedom to do this, or in other words his God-given task, he has to do this for its own sake, without having to ask anxiously what effect it will have on other people, whether it is in agreement with the confession of faith, or whether the church authorities will find it agreeable? In this sense the freedom of biblical criticism can be grounded upon the character of the Gospel itself. Naturally this, like all manifestations of justification by faith, has a certain conceptual and also historical relationship with secularism: where Christian freedom is withheld or is not seen as a good, then secularism as the best approximation is to be welcomed and supported. In these respects the spiritual and intellectual basis of biblical criticism can be seen to lie within the basic theological insights of the Reformation.

Biblical criticism developed the heritage of the Reformation in other respects also. In the Middle Ages text, interpretation, theology, and metaphysics formed, for many, one unitary body of knowledge, with an infinite network of interrelations between these different strata. Allegorical interpretation bound the details of the text and the convictions of theology and metaphysics together.[8] The Reformation questioned the harmony in which all this knowledge was supposed to stand. As against the synthesis of the later Middle Ages, a global picture of reality which looked as if it had

---

[7] For this paragraph I wish to acknowledge the stimulus of conversation with Dr. Robert Jewett.

[8] A full discussion of the nature of allegory must be left aside at this point.

always been so, the Reformers were easily able to show that this or that doctrinal element, far from having been there from eternity, had not been there in the Fathers, still less in the New Testament. The effect of this was to split up the global picture of reality into one involving temporally successive strata: in other words, it was a historical-critical operation, and one without which the Reformational position could not have sustained itself. When essentially the same approach came to be applied to the Bible, it was Protestantism rather than Roman Catholicism that was at first affected. Along with this shift of emphasis there went the questioning and restriction of allegorical interpretation, and the corresponding insistence upon the 'plain sense' of scripture.[9] The meaning of biblical texts was no longer necessarily coherent with scholastic teaching, or with Greek philosophy, or with accepted ecclesiastical doctrine: the texts, taken for themselves, could mean something substantially different. There was, from the Renaissance on, a certain distance between questions of different orders, and in particular between questions of the proximate meaning of texts on the one hand, and questions of the ultimate meaning of the universe on the other. The full recognition of this belongs, we may say, to the Enlightenment. Literary genres and the historical role of a writing can be discussed without *immediate* involvement in the ultimate questions of reality. Belief in the Incarnation does not tell us how Matthew was related to Luke, and belief in the Trinity does not tell us whether St Paul wrote the letter to the Ephesians or not. A certain *space* is created between the literary and historical questions on the one side and the ultimate theological decisions on the other. Moreover, on the other hand, the practice of historical reading seemed to be tied up with the character of the Christian faith itself. The reduction of confidence in a scholastic universe in which text, interpretation, and metaphysic were understood to interpenetrate each other had the effect that the actual saving events were all the more thrown into the foreground. It had always been understood in Christianity, but the Reformation had

---

[9] Protestantism of course developed its own allegory also; nevertheless the Protestant rejection of allegory remains a deeply significant factor.

made it even clearer, that the Christian faith depended on events which had taken place at some time in history. If this was so, it seemed to follow that it was important to know what the actual events, and their sequence, had been. Did Jesus cleanse the temple of the money-changers at the beginning of his ministry, as in John, or almost at the end, after his final entry into Jerusalem, as in the other Gospels? In the Middle Ages the question might have seemed not very important; but after the Reformation it was a serious matter. And, since the difference in point of fact between the two placings of this event seemed impossible to overcome, did not the difference lead to conclusions about the nature of the Gospels as literature and as historical reporting? Consider all these various influences together, and one cannot avoid the conclusion: it was the dynamics of Reformation theology that created the needs which biblical criticism was developed to answer. Take that great Protestant principle, the 'plain sense of scripture', and add to it that other great guide to understanding, namely that one should 'compare scripture with scripture': where do these lead but to what Wellhausen, among others, did?[10]

Again, biblical criticism followed Reformational exegesis in emphasizing what the biblical text *actually said*, the linguistic and grammatical datum of the text with the semantic implications of that datum. It is important to realize this, because hostile critics of biblical criticism have tended to represent it as if its criterion lay in so-called 'critical methods', in schemes, theories, and approaches which have been worked out in isolation and then imposed upon the text. In particular, many have supposed that under biblical criticism the science of history and its methods were given control over the Bible. On the contrary, the criterion for biblical criticism is, and always has been, *what the Bible itself actually says*. Of

[10] In saying this I do not ignore that there was a certain slippage in the sense of terms like 'plain sense'; on this cf. Childs's article on 'Sensus Literalis'. I neither appeal to the Reformation nor do I suggest that critical understandings of meaning were identical with, or even close to, Reformational understandings. Clearly the meaning of a term like 'plain sense' will alter as systems of ideas generally alter. As a matter of the history of ideas I think that the connections I have stated remain entirely valid. Childs's article seems to me to contain some wrong assessments of the facts; cf. my article on Jowett in *Horizons in Biblical Theology*.

course, biblical criticism has thrown up a bewildering variety of *theories*: like all forms of serious research, it operates through a considerable use of hypothesis. Hypotheses were generated, generally speaking, because there were data and relations in the texts which no one had hitherto properly explained; and the criterion for the acceptance or rejection of a hypothesis lay always, and must lie, in the evidence of the texts. This is an important point in the understanding and evaluation of biblical criticism. The existence of a hypothetical and reconstructive element in criticism has been an important element in modern reactions against it. It is proper therefore, to stress that critical theories, hypotheses, and methods have never been regarded by major exponents of biblical criticism as being themselves the criterion of judgement: it was always the text that was the criterion.[11]

The problem of scripture lies, however, not so much in the factual detailed material as in the organization or structure to be found within the whole. The factual material may function as the criterion for constructions of the total organization, but does not in itself provide such constructions. The meaning of scripture is seen when we organize its material in a certain way, or when we see that it is itself organized in a certain way. Theologies can thus be seen as attempts to organize scriptural materials in a meaningful way, giving higher importance to some aspects and lower to others, taking some elements as necessarily literal and assigning a more figurative or illustrative function to others. In this respect biblical criticism, when it emerged, was not essentially different: it can be said to have added another mode of organization, commonly a historical one, one expressed in terms of before and after; or, more accurately, it may be said to have refined and made much more important a mode of organization which in rudimentary form had always been there. The various forms of study, historical analysis, biblical theology, studies of the theology of individual writers like Luke or John, dogmatic theology,

[11] The hypothetical element in biblical criticism is undoubtedly one of the factors behind the rise of sympathy for new lines of study such as canonical criticism: the text as it stands, it is supposed, is hard evidence. Actually the products of canonical criticism so far fully share the hypothetical weaknesses of biblical criticism and often exceed them.

and philosophical theology can be regarded as attempts to provide or to identify structures and organizations within scripture, or bearing upon scripture, at different levels of detail and extension.

This character of theologies as organizations makes the working of scriptural authority more complicated. What is the relation of these structures to the total body of scriptural material? The common procedure seems to be thus: certain elements in scripture are picked out and taken as essential framework for the organization, which is then re-applied to the reading of the scripture as a whole. How then does this relate to the canon of scripture? Can the canon of scripture function as its own principle of organization, and should it so function? Some might argue thus: everything within the canon is vitally important and must be given its own place within the structure; it is not for man to pick and choose, to decide what is more and what is less important. This logic would at first sight seem to explain why the total inspiration of the whole is so emphasized, and with it the strictness of the boundary that separates the inspired scripture from the non-inspired other writings.

This is a reasonable argument in theory, but it works in fact in the opposite direction from that which people suppose. Traditional and orthodox theologies seldom worked according to the proportions of the biblical material; on the contrary, they commonly elevated to a key position in their structures elements which had comparatively slight and even marginal representation within the biblical material: the virgin birth, predestination, the inspiration of scripture.[12] The doing of this can be justified by a good theological argument; but it cannot be justified on the grounds that one is following the proportions dictated by the canonical material of scripture itself, it can only be justified on the quite other grounds that there is, buried within scripture or even known from

---

[12] Traditional orthodoxy related to the canon as exact boundary of inspiration not because it represented correctly the proportions of material within the canon, but for the quite contrary reason that it depended upon elements which were thinly represented in the canon and which therefore could be validated only on the grounds that anything within the canon, however thinly evidenced, was completely inspired and therefore usable as part of an essential theological structure.

without it, a set of key elements which have overriding theological authority, such as to give them an importance going far beyond the representation of them in the canonical material. In this sense traditional orthodoxy is a monumental example of the 'picking and choosing' that it deprecates in others. Actually, 'liberal' theology in its emphasis on (say) the Kingdom of God was following the canonical proportions of the Gospels much more faithfully. Modern biblical theologies can be seen as serious attempts to work out the organization or structure that is presented by the proportions of the biblical material itself, and in this respect may be judged to have been relatively successful.[13] But in principle two points should be recognized: firstly, the character of theologies as organizations means that scripture, just taken in itself, does not necessarily generate its own theology or the true theology. Theologies that are built upon the equal inspiration of all scripture, or upon the precise boundaries of the canon, are not less operations of selection and emphasis than are other theologies.[14] Secondly, and conversely, the canon of scripture, as canon, does not provide organizational guidance for the construction of theologies, and was never intended to do so—a point to which we shall return.[15]

Many churches have some kind of 'stepped canon', as Judaism has: that is to say, certain books are taken as more central, others as more peripheral, and this is exhibited in some way. In Lutheranism, as is well known, there is a heavy stress upon the central Pauline letters, and correspondingly certain books, like James, Hebrews, and Revelation, were placed in an appendix. In many currents of Anglicanism the supreme position is accorded to the Gospels: the congregation sits to hear the Old Testament and the Epistle, but stands for the Gospel. These practices are a very rough and approximate indication of the point we have just been making, namely that

---

[13] In this respect the movement of modern biblical theology can be rather warmly defended against the constant allegation of Childs that it neglected the canon of scripture: it actually observed the lines and proportions of canonical scripture rather well, and its weaknesses have to be sought elsewhere.

[14] Fundamentalism, for instance, is an operation of picking and choosing, in which some things are emphasized, others de-emphasized, some taken literally, others left as marginal; see my *Fundamentalism* (London: SCM, 2nd edn., 1981).

[15] See below, pp. 67–70.

a theology constructs an organization out of the total biblical material. Some might object to the introduction of any such distinction between one set of books and another within the canon, and that also can be understood. But fundamentally it makes no difference, for in any case an organization has to be constructed, or accepted as being already there: a church that takes the canon as one level piece, without steps or distinctions, must still make its own balance between what is more central and what is more peripheral. The more modern formulation of a similar question, that is, whether there is, or should be, a 'canon within the canon', will be discussed later.[16]

Finally, some thoughts about the linkage between the community and the canon of scripture, about the *effect* which the existence of a canon has upon the understanding. One interesting view is the idea that the canon constitutes part of the self-definition of the church. 'For a community to call itself "church" is to say, *inter alia*, that it is a community whose continuing self-identity depends on the use, not just (vaguely) of some writings, but *precisely use of just these writings*.'[17] The canon is analytic in the judgement 'this community is a church'.

It is hard, however, to take this argument seriously in the form in which it stands. Perhaps it might be more positively stated in this form: that the existence and recognition of *a scripture* is part of the self-definition of the church. A scripture is something different from '(vaguely) some writings'; but it is also different from the canon, i.e. the definition of the precise boundary of the scripture. The church of biblical times certainly had a scripture, but it is by no means clear that it had a canon in the sense of a precise definition of the books, indeed it is highly probable that it did not.[18] More widely, however, it should be clear that the identity of church communities is not constituted by the precise contents of their canon. On the contrary, changes in the canon would probably have little or no effect in so far as they concerned the marginal books of the canon; or, conversely, one may

---

[16] See below, pp. 70–73.
[17] D.H. Kelsey, *The Uses of Scripture in Recent Theology* (London: SCM, 1975), p. 105; cf. my review in *Virginia Seminary Journal* 1978–9, 40.
[18] See below, pp. 61ff.

designate books as 'marginal' in exactly this respect, namely, that their presence within the canon, or their omission from it, makes and would make little or no difference to the identity of the church community and its faith and practice. No one could reasonably suppose that the self-identity of the Roman Catholic church would be materially affected if it dropped the Book of Ecclesiasticus from its canon, or even if it dropped all the books which Protestants have traditionally counted as Apocrypha. Nor would Protestant communities be materially changed if Ecclesiasticus or Wisdom were to be read in them as Old Testament lessons. Such changes would cause a stir because they were changes and because they implied a shift in the status of holy books; but beyond this they would not affect the actual shape and identity of the church, and its faith would not be altered.

The reason for this is the fact that there is no direct correlation between the self-identity of a church and the *precise* boundaries of its canon. There is little or nothing specific in the Book of Wisdom that is directly essential to the self-identity of the Roman Catholic church; and there is little or nothing in the content of Wisdom or Ecclesiasticus that is more remote from the self-identity of a traditional Protestant church than the material of the canonical book of Proverbs. The amount of the specific identity-forming doctrines and practices of Catholicism and Orthodoxy that derived specifically from the 'apocryphal' books was minute in comparison with the contribution of other factors, and conversely the amount of the distinct Protestant position that was specifically dictated by the Protestant rejection of the Apocrypha was also minute.[19] Conversely, nearly all the widely-differing Protestant churches had the same canon, but this did not alter

[19] The traditional example, namely the citation of 2 Macc. 12:38–45 as evidence for the practice of intercession and expiation for the dead, and even for the notion of Purgatory, illustrates this well. The classic controversy over this presupposed a simple proof-text approach to doctrine which few or none on either side would maintain today. Catholic views about these matters would doubtless have developed in any case, even if 2 Maccabees had not been considered canonical or had not existed at all. Protestants, even if they had accepted the book as canonical, could have argued that the practices and attitudes in question were merely an outmoded aspect of Judaism, like many practices and attitudes of the (canonical) Old Testament. The basis for the Protestant position lay not in the rejection of the

the fact of the deep diversities and splits between them, their greatly differing self-identities.

The functioning of the canon seems to me to lie rather in the opposite direction. Far from the canon establishing or expressing the self-identity of the church, it is the church that establishes the network of familiar relations within which its scriptures are known and understood. This may or may not have been part of the motive for the setting up of a canon, but it seems to be the way in which the existence of the canon has worked, especially in the more recent centuries. If books are canonical, although they come from ancient times and unfamiliar cultures, they are continually read, studied, expounded, and (though in varying degree) used in the life of liturgy and prayer. Other works that come from these same ancient times and unfamiliar cultures, though they may express substantially the same faith and religion, come to be unknown: they are historical monuments, read only by scholars and specialists. The church thus provides for its canonical scriptures a sort of hermeneutic updating: familiarity with precisely *these* texts provides the frame of reference for understanding. People may not succeed in understanding but they know what it is that they ought to be understanding, or trying to understand, if they take their religion seriously, and it is these books, 'the Bible', that have clear and special association with their own present-day church. But this is true only of canonical scriptures. Canonical scripture is the Word of God, as heard within the church of today. It forms a special circle of its own. The books are not encapsulated within their own original culture and history but have a special status. Other books are not read in the same way, even if they, as it may be, express Christian beliefs more precisely. St. Augustine's *Confessions* are much closer to the mind, the concepts, and the culture of the modern Christian than is the Gospel of

canonicity of 2 Maccabees, but in the overpowering conviction that intercessions and expiatory practices for the dead were illegitimate; the roots of this conviction, however, lie elsewhere in the total network of the Protestant consciousness. The fact that there was, within the canonical New Testament, a reference to 'baptism for the dead'—whatever exactly that may mean—at 1 Cor. 15:29, where the practice, though not commended, is not forbidden, was not sufficient to overcome this deeply-rooted conviction.

St. Mark, but St. Mark is read directly, for the Word of God coming through it, St. Augustine for the thoughts of a man of late antiquity, one who indeed interprets well the Word of God, but one whom one reads through the same process with which one would read another book by a Christian of that time. St. Augustine is thus farther away: for canonical scripture distance does not really matter.[20] So at any rate it seems to have worked in traditional Christianity.

That this is so only for canonical scriptures is most easily to be seen if one looks at books which are canonical in one communion but not in another. To the average Protestant Christian the book of Daniel is part of his church setting; he may not understand it, he may not even have read it, but he recognizes it as part of the context which he acknowledges, and it belongs in the same circle with the other books of which he knows, with Genesis, with Isaiah, with the Gospels. But if he looks at Enoch he does not feel this way at all: the remoteness, the lack of power to communicate, the distance in another world and another culture, immediately strike him. But there is no such feeling about Enoch in the Ethiopian church, because it has long been canonical there. Our western canon includes Chronicles, which is a rewrite of Samuel-Kings, and we accept the coexistence of both without a thought; but it does not include Jubilees, which is a rewrite of Genesis-Exodus, and Jubilees is to us a remote and immensely strange universe. Thus, reading Genesis or Isaiah, the western Christian may probably ask himself 'what is this saying to me today?', but on reading Enoch or Jubilees he is not likely even to ask the question. But this is not because of the intrinsic merits or demerits of the books: it is because the books are canonical and uncanonical respectively.

If books which we now consider canonical had not been canonical, we would in many cases not easily have seen any reason why they should be canonical. Who would have argued for the canonization of Chronicles, if it had in fact descended to us in a status like that of Jubilees? If Ecclesiastes had not in fact been canonical, no one would ever have

---

[20] One can of course read the Fathers as an extension of the canon or as a secondary canon; but this only moves the same question to a different point.

dreamt of the salutary contributions to Christian doctrine that its presence is supposed to furnish. The logic of canonicity favours whatever has come to be canonical and disfavours whatever has not. Intrinsic religious value is made subsidiary to this consideration. If a book—say Esther—is canonical, then it does not require to be validated on the grounds of religious merit, for it is an inspired and canonical text, and this fact overrides considerations of intrinsic religious merit. But this principle does not work equally in reverse: uncanonical texts are commonly depreciated because their religious content is poor, something that would not happen if these same texts were canonical.

These things are more obvious in the more marginal texts like Esther and Ecclesiastes, Enoch and Jubilees; but something similar could apply even in more central books. Suppose, for instance, that the protests against the Johannine literature had been successful,[21] and John had not continued in the New Testament canon: we would have had by now nearly seventeen hundred years of Christian faith with the Synoptic Gospels but without John; and, trained in this long tradition, we would have found John exceedingly strange, rather heretical in tendency, something like some of the apocryphal gospels are to some of us. Supposing that the Diatessaron had won the day and superseded the separate gospels: we would have had one single and combined gospel, and no doubt many would consider it an absurd speculation that scholars would claim to find within this one gospel a 'Matthew source' and a 'John source', when everyone knew that the gospel was only one single book. The fourfold separate gospels, as we now have them, would have seemed a strange and rather improper version.

This leads us to a few concluding remarks. Firstly, one must wonder whether the great question as posed by twentieth-century biblical hermeneutics was not wrongly conceived. It was often said that, given our knowledge of the original historical meaning of texts, the great hermeneutical task was to enable us to move from there to the meaning for today, to show how in some sense this could be meaningful

---

[21] On the anti-Johannine movement see Campenhausen, pp. 238ff.

and relevant for the life of the church today, how it could be seen also as an effective Word of God. Was this not an immense straining to accomplish something that was actually there all the time? Was not the special status of scripture both given and accepted throughout, in spite of the new angles introduced by modern criticism? Was not the real question this: not, given the historical meaning, how do we move from it to the meaning as Word of God for today, but, given the church's readiness to hear the scripture as Word of God for today, how is that hearing to be modified, refined, and clarified through our knowledge of the actual character of the biblical text, as mediated through critical, historical, and other sorts of knowledge?

Secondly we should observe that the essential dynamics of the canon do not appear to vary as between Catholic and Protestant traditions. The Roman canon includes some more books but it also knows the existence of apocrypha, of books which have come near to acceptance but have not in the end been accepted: the Clementine Vulgate prints Fourth Ezra, along with some other pieces, within the Latin Bible but in an appendix at the end. But, compared with Protestant ortho-doxy, for which there had to be a quite absolute division between inspired and non-inspired books, the Roman posi-tion probably leaves more room for a grey area, a group of books which are marginal but come close to full canonicity; and this is certainly true of the Anglican position. The decision about the marginal books is not, in the last resort, a very important question; and the major dynamics of the canon operate whatever answer we give to that question.

We began by observing that there is an important difference between the situation where the Bible already stood complete as an acknowledged and delimited canon, and the situation of the men of the Bible themselves. Some part of the latter situation was fairly evident even from the biblical text as it stands, but much of it was hidden and could be perceived only through a reconstruction, a reconstruction which asked what had actually happened, what had been said and at what time, and in what order events had developed. It was critical scholarship that undertook that reconstruction. In this sense it is responsible for recovering much of what can be known of the situation of the men of the Bible themselves. It is true, of course, that most of our evidence for this reconstruction is to be found within the text of scripture itself. But the evidence is not always to be seen if the scripture is read straightforwardly *as canon*, as it stands, seen purely in the light of the surface relations of the text. For it is one of the marked characteristics of scripture, caused by the way in which the materials were formed into scripture, that it conceals the circumstances of its own making. The effect of tradition becoming scripture was to foreshorten the tradition, within the biblical period, to an astonishing degree. Precisely because it became scripture, and because practically no extra-scriptural tradition from the biblical period survived, scripture when read just as it stands conceals much of the way in which it itself has come to be. The case of Moses is a good example. Ancient Israel contained law which developed over a long period as the society changed. Some of it was ancient customary law, which must have existed long before Moses is supposed to have lived. Other elements came, perhaps, with Moses, others with the Deuteronomic reforms in the eighth and seventh centuries, others still later. As I have said, it was in the Deuteronomic stage that it came to be insisted that the 'book of the law' given to Moses is the central foundation for Israel's legal constitution. The effect was that, as all the law from different periods was brought together, the way of giving it maximum status was to associate it with Moses. The reader who simply reads this material can see it as one book, given at one time by one man, with no legal development to be seen in Israel at all. Only if the details are carefully studied and a *critical* reading undertaken is it possible to penetrate behind the text and see something of how things were in Israel in biblical times.

When traditional Christianity affirmed the authority of the Bible it did not make it clear whether this meant the authority of the books as such or the authority of the people, the time, the life of the Bible. Perhaps the question did not arise in any sharp fashion. But we today can hardly avoid putting it. It no longer makes sense to speak of the authority of the Bible as if it meant the authority of the written documents, quite apart from the persons and lives that lie behind them. Authority must belong to both: certainly to the books, but not only to the books. Romans is authoritative because St. Paul is authoritative, and still more the Gospels have authority because of Jesus Christ, the person and his life, of which they tell. Christianity as a faith is not directed in the first place towards a book, but towards the persons within and behind that book and the life of the ancient community which was their context and in which they made themselves known. Critical biblical study, in making known something more of that life and those persons, is thus—at the very least—contributing directly towards the understanding of the basis of authority that underlies the church. The church is founded 'upon the foundation of the apostles and prophets' (Eph. 2:20), not upon the foundation of the books named after them. The pre-Christian basis of the church, though by shorthand we often call it the Old Testament, is in fact Israel;[22] analogously, what we call the New Testament, is really, as a basis for Christianity, Jesus and his life, the community which he founded and its leadership.

---

[22] I here follow the fine words of H. Berkhof, *Christian Faith* (Grand Rapids: Eerdmans, 1979), p. 221: 'What we call Israel here is usually called the Old Testament in the Christian church.... In this chapter we shall constantly speak about the Old Testament. But deviating from usual practice, we make this name subordinate to the name Israel. For here we are not concerned with the book as such, but with the faith and the history of the people of Israel to which this book bears witness.' It is 'Israel' therefore, and not the Old Testament, that is the primary object of theological reflection. I think this is entirely right, and very important. Dutch original, *Christelijk Geloof* (Nijkerk: Callenbach, 1973), p. 234.

III

The concept of canon and its modern adventures

When we talk about a canon of scripture, we refer in the first place to the fact that the Bible contains certain books, while others are outside the canon and do not count as holy scripture. If we take a really strict old-fashioned view of inspiration, all books within the canon are fully inspired by the Holy Spirit, and no books outside it, however good in other respects, are inspired. The word 'canon' meant simply 'list', i.e. the list of books that counted as holy scripture.[1] The following remarks will concern mainly the canon of the Old Testament, and also the view of it as seen from the perspective of later Judaism and the New Testament; the canon of the New Testament itself will be more marginally considered.

The Hebrew Bible, as is well known, is disposed in three steps or stages, the Law, the Prophets, and the Writings. The distinction between Former and Latter Prophets, i.e. between the 'historical books' (as we often call them) Joshua-Kings and the prophetic books Isaiah-Malachi, is late and does not

[1] This is, and has always been, the normal meaning of the word in English when applied to scripture. It derives from the familiar Greek sense, as used of a table of figures or the like; similarly, in ecclesiastical usage, saints are 'canonized' when they are included in the catalogue of saints. Cf. *Oxford Dictionary of the Christian Church* under the various words 'canon'. Some other ways in which the term has come to be used in modern canonical criticism will be mentioned below, ch. 4. It is important to observe that 'canon' in the sense of 'canon of scripture' thus appears not to derive from the sense 'rule, standard', which is the New Testament sense of the Greek word. In some recent theological discussion new usages of the word 'canon' have proliferated. One hears that an *event* can be a canon; and one hears a usage in which the term 'canon' seems to be supposed to have a higher status that 'scripture' does, so that 'scripture' means more or less the Bible with its special qualities but 'canon' is the proper term for 'scripture when seen as authoritative in the community'. Such usage is a regrettable innovation, without secure basis in traditional theological language; moreover, it is confusing to the point of being nonsensical. If we mean 'scripture when seen as authoritative in the community' we should say 'scripture when seen as authoritative in the community', and not confuse ourselves by calling it 'canon'.

come into the historical range of our survey; nevertheless it forms a useful distinction which we may at times use, anachronistically, where the distinction is important. Now the usual view, familiar from standard works of reference, is that these three sections were 'canonized' in that same order: first the Torah, about the fifth century BC perhaps, then the Prophets by about 200, and finally the Writings. Some think that the Writings must already have been fixed as a canon in Maccabaean times, i.e. in the second century BC, others think that it was not done until late in the first century AD, in other words after Christianity was already on the scene. It is easy to think, also, that the difference of sequence corresponds to a difference of importance: for there is no question that in Judaism the Torah is immensely preponderant, while some of the Writings play a comparatively unimportant role in the religious structure.

If there is something faulty in this conception, it may start with the notion of 'canon' itself. The word 'canon' is a Christian term; moreover, when used in this sense, it is a rather late Christian term, not found until about the fourth century AD.[2] There seems to be no ancient Hebrew expression meaning 'canon'; not that this in itself proves anything, but at least it indicates that there is reason for caution in defining what is being discussed. In the Hebrew Bible, as a matter of fact, there is not really a word for 'scripture' either. Now there are various rabbinic expressions about books that may or may not 'make the hands unclean', and these are found in rabbinic discussions about certain books, such as Song of Songs and Ecclesiastes, in the later first century AD. The point has often been taken to be this: holy books made the hands 'unclean', in the sense that after handling them one had to undergo certain ritual purifications before doing certain other things. When the rabbis discussed, therefore, whether Ecclesiastes made the hands unclean, people have understood this to mean that they

---

[2] See Lampe, *A Patristic Greek Lexicon* (Oxford: Clarendon Press, 1961), p. 701. The Greek καυών is of course found in the New Testament but there it means a 'standard' or 'rule', and this probably belongs to a quite different semantic department of the word. I do not suggest that the late date for the first use of the word καυών in the sense of 'canon' shows that the idea of the canon was lacking earlier; nevertheless the late date is significant, for it indicates how slow and gradual was the conceptualization and lexicalization of this idea.

were discussing whether or not it was a canonical book, and thought this therefore to imply that it had not yet been decided whether it was canonical or not. This may be right but there are other interpretations. It is surely more likely that the question is a truly ritual one: the discussion is not, whether this or that book is canonical, but whether it, canonical or not, had certain ritual effects. It is therefore uncertain whether this matter of 'making the hands unclean' really refers directly to canonicity, and uncertain whether it forms evidence concerning the date of closing of the 'canon'. It seems to me possible that terms have been thoughtlessly transferred from the *Christian* history of the canon: since the Christian New Testament went through a canonization process, people have thought that the same should be true of the Jewish Bible. But this is not necessarily so: there are important differences in the situation and in the problems. The Old Testament materials were a national literature, much of it nationally known and recognized from an early time. The existence of parallel-running books covering the same ground, which was central to the growth of the idea of a canonical group of four gospels, was probably of little importance. Again, it is doubtful whether the motive of defining the accepted books in order to exclude heretical or unorthodox books was very important. The processes were very different and it is not clear that we do right to talk about a 'canonization' process for the Hebrew Bible at all.

In particular is this the case with the Torah. The Torah was never 'canonized'. No process of listing, or of choosing as against competing books, or of excluding others, was involved. The Torah could be counted as one single book, the Law of Moses, in five sections which read in sequence. What happened was that this book, or an earlier stage of it, became supremely authoritative in the religious and legal sphere. It was not seriously challenged and it had no real competitors. Thus the attainment by the Torah of central and definitive status was not really a process of canonization. If we ask how and when this happened, James Sanders has pointed to the important fact of the intrusion of Deuteronomy between Numbers and Joshua: where previously there had been a sequential story that ran on from the travels in the desert to the conquest of the Holy Land, there was now a further book of Law which rounded off the Pentateuch and separated it from the story of events after Moses' death, with great consequent effects on the religion thereafter.[3]

In itself this may be quite right but I think the essential step was taken not by the form of the books but by the *ideas* of Deuteronomy. For, as has been mentioned,[4] it was this book that insisted that 'this law', 'this book of the Torah', should be decisive for all questions, should be studied daily by kings (Deut. 17:18ff.) and so on; and it was the acceptance of this ideal, plus the accumulation of yet more legal materials within the Mosaic tradition and the consequent completion of the *text* of the Pentateuch, that formed the essential shape of Jewish religion as it was to be. The essential thing was not so much the separation between the books of Moses and Joshua-Judges, but the acceptance of the principle that the Mosaic law was completely paramount. When did this happen? Tradition associates it with Ezra. Though it is difficult to make this association precise, it is a good general indication. The full predominance of the Torah, seen as Mosaic law, comes from about the fifth century: it is still not there in Jeremiah, in Ezekiel, or in the latter parts of the Book of Isaiah; in Ezra-Nehemiah, however, in rough terms it is already there.

Now, if the Torah was not really 'canonized', what about the Prophets? It is not certain that they were canonized either. When, in the fifth century or earlier, the Torah became religiously paramount, there was already in existence a great deal of religiously authoritative national literature. Of this there were two great blocks. The first is the sequential story, originally starting from the beginning of the world and going down to around the Babylonian Exile; the first part of this story had by now, however, been absorbed into the Law of Moses, and what remained was later to be known as 'The Former Prophets'. The second block was the set of books named after prophets (later the 'Latter Prophets'). The religious recognition of much of this material may have been

---

[3] J.A. Sanders, *Torah and Canon* (Philadelphia: Fortress Press, 1972); many of the details of his reconstruction, however, seem speculative to me.
[4] Cf. above, p. 7.

earlier than the recognition of the supremacy of the Torah; the effect of the latter was that this other material, already religiously authoritative, continued to have that recognition, but necessarily in a position less dominant than the Torah. This analysis is, indeed, not far different from the basic classic understanding of Wellhausen, in its placing of the Law in relation to the Prophets. On the other hand it places the recognition (in customary terms 'canonization') of the Prophets earlier than has commonly been supposed.[5]

One historical note should be added here. The older discussion was rather over-persuaded by the case of the Samaritans, whose scripture includes only the Torah and not the Prophets. This has long been supposed to be evidence that the Prophets were 'canonized' only after the separation of Samaritans from Jews. But it could also be understood, on the terms of the position I have just taken, by supposing that the move to absolutize the Torah, which was highly effective among the Jews, was even more complete among the Samaritans, to the point that they let the Prophets drop quite out of the status of 'scripture'. This may well have been the case in some Jewish groups also. Moreover, although Samaritan 'scripture' is limited to the Torah, the Samaritan Chronicles evince considerable influence from the non-Torah books, notably in the high importance attached to the person of Eli. If the Samaritans had simply 'closed their canon' with no contents in it other than the Torah, it is difficult to see how all this other material would have gained entrance, even only as an influence. It is more probable that we should understand Samaritanism as having had a recognition of the material of some of the 'prophets' from an early time, having imposed the Torah as completely dominant over this, but even thereafter having accepted influence from the other books.[6] In any case recent studies suggest that the 'schism' between Jews and Samaritans was considerably later than

[5] The dating of materials in this way, however, is not essential to the general position I take about the canon of the Old Testament, and that position could be asserted with small variations if this dating had to be discarded.

[6] See in general R.J. Coggins, *Samaritans and Jews* (Oxford: Blackwell, 1975) and R. Pummer, 'The Present State of Samaritan Studies', *JSS* 21, 1976, 39–61; 22, 1977, 27–47.

used to be supposed; and if it was very late then one could no longer say that the Samaritans did not accept the Prophets because the Jews at that time had not yet accepted them as 'canonical' either.

We return, then, to the position of the non-Torah material, the 'Prophets'. Why, we may ask, was all this material designated as 'Prophets'? Naturally, this term fits for the large collections of books named after prophets, the Latter Prophets as they came to be called. But it is not so clear how it applies to what we call the historical books. We have to look not at the form or the contents of the books as we now see them, but at the way in which they were then regarded. It might be held that the prophets who appear from time to time in the historical books were the real religious teachers of the period and therefore supplied the essential content. Or, again, the story of the historical books could be understood as interlinked with predictive prophecy, so that the past history made sense through the presence of indications of the future, which indications showed in what direction that past was going. Or, again, something may have come from the anachronistic generalizing attitude which made all great religious figures of ancient times into 'prophets', so that David was a 'prophet', just as before him Noah and Abraham had been 'prophets'. Or, again, because the entire block (the 'Prophets') included undeniable books by prophets (the 'Latter Prophets' in later parlance), the name might just have spread by semantic extension to the whole, without anyone worrying about the appropriateness of the terms.

If this is so, why then were yet other books, which were also part of Israel's heritage of religious literature, not also included among the 'prophets'? The answer is that they probably were. In other words, it may well be that there was not a closed 'canon' of the Prophets, to which there was later added a further 'canon' of the Writings; instead of the three-stage organization familiar to us, there probably was for a considerable time a two-stage conception, using only the two terms, the Torah and the 'Prophets'. Some books, which to us are in the Writings, may well have been in the Prophets: the obvious case is the Psalms, written by that well-known prophet, David. In 2 Macc. 15:9, where Judas Maccabaeus encourages his troops with passages from 'the law and the prophets', it could mean, as some interpreters have understood it, that the Law and the Prophets as we know them were then canonical but not the Writings as we know them; but it could more probably mean that 'the Prophets' for 2 Maccabees included some books which later came to count as Writings. It is quite likely, for instance, that Judas included among the passages encouraging his troops the first verse of Ps. 68, 'Let God arise, let his enemies be scattered'. And most familiarly, of course, this agrees with the situation in the New Testament itself, where we never hear explicitly of the threefold division into Law, Prophets, and Writings: the nearest we come to it is Lk. 24:44 where we hear of 'the Law of Moses, the Prophets and Psalms', which might possibly imply the threefold division. In the New Testament, however, the normal classification is into the two simple categories, the Law and the Prophets. This strongly suggests that the category of 'Prophet' was not a closed one: any non-Torah book that was holy scripture was a 'Prophet'. Josephus, similarly, gives precise numbers for the books in each of three groups, and thus he appears on the face of it to have a tripartite canon, and his total set of books probably agrees with that of our Hebrew Bible; but his numbers can be made to fit only on the assumption that he included in his group of 'Prophets' several books which to us are among the Writings (Esther, Chronicles, Job, Daniel?). Thus with Josephus, even if the total set of books is identical with the present Jewish canon, the division of membership between the Prophets and the other books is certainly different, and is a little bit more like the arrangement we find in the texts of the Septuagint.[7] Indeed it is conceivable that Josephus does not really have a three-stage canon at all, but a two-stage one, namely (1) the Books of Moses (2) a. the succeeding history, from the death of Moses to Artaxerxes king of Persia, written by prophets, and b. books of hymns and precepts, also written by prophets. The text could be read in this way. In any case it seems likely

---

[7] This rather considerable agreement between Josephus's enumeration and the arrangement of books in the LXX is a reason against the view, now gaining ground, that there was no Jewish 'Alexandrian canon' apart from the Pentateuch; see below, p. 56.

that, although the separate status of the Torah was clear, the boundary between the Prophets and other books was fluid, still vague, and possibly quite unimportant in the first century AD.

Two historical points should here be added, not so much in the hope of settling them, but rather in order to pass on information about the recent trends of scholarship. Firstly, it has often been thought that, late in the first century AD, after the fall of Jerusalem, a 'council' or 'synod' took place at Jamnia, that it included these discussions about the making unclean of the hands, and that this constituted the final closing of the biblical canon for Jews. It has more recently been argued that there was no such council or synod at all, that these discussions were academic discussions about legal questions and were not in themselves a matter of the closing of the canon. Therefore, as far as this argument goes, the canon could have been closed earlier; more important, evidence about discussions at Jamnia does not show us how or through what sort of decisions the canon came to be closed at all.

Secondly, it has been generally thought that the Egyptian Jews had a wider canon, including books that in Palestine never became canonical. This larger canon is represented by our texts of the Septuagint. When the church took over the Old Testament, it took it over in the form of this wider Alexandrian canon.[8] Against this it has more recently been strongly argued that there was no 'Alexandrian canon': the only canon at Alexandria was the Torah and, in addition to it, according to Sundberg, there was no 'canon' but a large, uncanonized corpus of holy books, 'a wide religious literature without definite bounds'. We shall not attempt here to give a final answer to these complicated questions; but it is clear that we can no longer *automatically* reckon with the idea of a larger 'Alexandrian canon'.

The question is posed particularly by the books that came eventually to be classed (by Jerome, and later by Protestants) as 'Apocrypha'—I think above all of Tobit, Wisdom of

---

[8] For a typical statement of the 'Alexandrian canon' theory see R.H. Pfeiffer in *IDB* i. 510–11; cf. also O. Eissfeldt, *The Old Testament* (Oxford: Blackwell, 1965), pp. 570–1.

Solomon, Ben Sira, Enoch, Jubilees—and by the writings more recently brought to our cognizance by Qumran. What sort of status did these have? When we look at this problem we see how unsatisfactory the idea of a 'canon' is, for it implies a clear distinction between scripture and non-scripture, inspired and non-inspired, divine and human, authoritative and non-authoritative, which very probably was not there. Sundberg's 'wide religious literature without definite bounds' is perhaps too vague, and yet perhaps gives a better impression that the idea of a 'canon'. Possibly we have to think of something more like a backbone, securely established, namely the Torah and most or all of the Prophets, plus the Psalms, and beyond that a placing of other books at greater or lesser proximity, some closer and some more remote.

Two or three further historical aspects should be mentioned. One small, almost physical, point is this: for us a Bible is a single volume bound together, and what is not in that volume is not scripture. The order is given by the order of pages in the volume. This, however, is a concept realizable only since the invention of the codex, and still more since the invention of the printed book. In biblical times the books were separate individual scrolls. A 'Bible' was not a volume one could hold in the hand, but a cupboard or chest with pigeonholes, or a room or cave with a lot of individual scrolls. The boundary between what was scripture, and what were other holy books, was thus more difficult to indicate, and so was the order of the books and the organization (if any) of the canon.

Moreover, we seldom have hard evidence about how questions of canon were decided, until late times. How does one fix or close a canon? Within Judaism, if the idea of the Jamnia council must be abandoned, we really have no information about meetings or councils of authorities which established these matters, and it is not clear indeed that there were institutions with the power or the means to do so. More probably, we may suggest, canons, in so far as such things existed, existed in the form of the different opinions of different groups; and a settlement was eventually reached not through a 'decision' but through the fact that one group became dominant, its opinion became more powerful and important, and other views simply faded away with the fading of the groups which had maintained them. It is quite likely that it happened so in Judaism, as it happened with the variant texts of the Bible: the great wars with the Romans obliterated certain deviant versions, and a single position, on canon as on text, was left in possession of the field. It is thus not surprising that the earliest texts showing an interest in the enumeration of the precise number of scriptural books come from the late first century AD at earliest: Josephus and Fourth Ezra. Josephus in setting out his enumeration of books insists that the number is precise and implies that it is accepted by all Jews: in spite of the long ages that have passed no one has added, removed, or altered a syllable. This is just what people think about the customs and institutions of their own group; it may well be that there were other groups that had thought differently, and that Josephus either did not know of their opinion, or conveniently forgot it.[9]

Moreover, we seldom know very well the grounds on which decisions about canonical questions were reached, and even when some grounds are mentioned it is often difficult to know whether they were the ones that were really effective. Sometimes views of the theological contribution that a book would make may have had an effect, but alongside this one has to put other factors, such as beliefs about the person who wrote it, the prestige of the communities in which it was revered, and so on. Arguments for and against the canonicity of books may in many cases be reasons after the fact, arguments for what has been done after it had already been done. A good example is Irenaeus's famous argument over the necessity that there should be precisely four Gospels, as there are four regions of the world, four winds, four faces of

---

[9] His argument is polemical and tendentious. Its point is the contrast with the Greeks. The Greeks have a multitude of inconsistent and conflicting books, the Jews have a limited number of consistent and reliable books. Even if Josephus was right and all Jews had been completely agreed about the canon, his argument would have been an unfair one, for he is comparing Greek literature and philosophy on one side with Jewish *scripture* on the other. Actually there were far more Jewish books than the limited set of biblical books. Or else, conversely, the Jewish scriptures might have been compared with the Iliad and Odyssey (twenty-four books each) or the works of Plato, equally enumerable and limited.

the cherubim: if, however, there had been three Gospels, e.g. if Mark had dropped out, one could (and no doubt would) have argued decisively that there could in the nature of things only be three gospels, since three is the number of the Holy Trinity, the number of the basic cosmic elements (heaven, earth, and sea), and Matthew might have been the Gospel of the Father, Luke of the Son, and John of the Spirit—who knows? Moreover, the fact that a writer or a theologian concerned himself with questions of the canon does not necessarily mean that they were very important to his basic thinking. They were to Irenaeus in his argument about the fourfold Gospel, but they were not always. Athanasius, for example, in his Festal Letter of 367 is said to furnish the first list which agrees precisely with the modern (Protestant) canon for the entire Bible, but it is not to be supposed on this ground that the canon was a very important matter in the basic creative theological thinking of Athanasius. It was not, and he continued to use as scriptural evidence passages from books that were not included in the canon list of his famous letter. The matter was of only marginal importance to the main issues of his theological thinking.

More important for our purpose, perhaps, is this further aspect: as I have repeatedly stressed, the situation of the later observer or theologian, for whom the canon of scripture is an accomplished fact, is quite different from that of the men of biblical times, for whom the completion of the canon, perhaps even the idea of a canon at all, still lay far in the future. Let us suppose that a Jew of the second century BC came upon a book, like the Book of Enoch, of deeply impressive learning, religious power, and devotion to the principles of Judaism. How could he decide about it? For, even if it was then not yet acknowledged that it was an inspired book, of divine origin, it might still be a potentially inspired book, a book of which it might in due course turn out that it was inspired and fully authoritative. In that situation—and it may have been normal during the time from about 200 BC to 100 AD—the concept of canon is of no use. It is not likely that people proceeded by the rational question, 'Shall we add this book to the canon?' There were already holy books, there was scripture, but it is not clear that there was a canon. The canon tells one, after the decisions have been made, what the decision was; but it is not an important or even a useful factor at the time when the decision has still to be made. In biblical times, and for some centuries in later Judaism, there was this category of books that might perhaps come to be scripture: one did not yet know, but the possibility was there. Enoch may well have been like this. It came from an environment and an ideology quite close to Daniel: Daniel was coming to be widely accepted, perhaps Enoch would be accepted too?

To this must be added another important point about the situation within Judaism. It is a natural supposition, and perhaps very roughly correct,[10] that the three-stage canon of the Hebrew Bible corresponds to decreasing degrees of religious authority and importance: the Torah was certainly dominant, the Prophets important, the Writings of only limited importance. The dominance of the Law is beyond question. But the rest of the gradation does not work out in detail. If we take the criterion of what is read in normal liturgical cycles, the Law is central, but the Prophets, Former and Latter as we call them, are read only in selections, and in some ways more importance attaches to the Megilloth or short books, Esther, Ruth, Song of Songs, Lamentations and Ecclesiastes, which are read at certain important festivals and are exceedingly familiar in Jewish life; certain of the Psalms are also exceedingly important. The main body of midrash, a deeply important Jewish genre, is also devoted to the Torah and the Megilloth. I would not assert that all these features go back as far as the beginnings of Christianity; but at least they are characteristic for Judaism as it has developed. Attention is not evenly spread over the entire body of scripture; but neither is it distributed according to the gradation of the threefold canon. If on the other hand we look for that which is essential for the proof of halachah or law, there is no question that the Torah is the sole major source. Philo of Alexandria quoted practically no authority other than the Pentateuch. The Mishnah quotes overwhelmingly from the Torah, and a certain amount from the Psalms and Proverbs, but extremely little from the historical books.

[10] Cf. above, p. 50.

More important still, however: in rabbinic Judaism, as it developed, there came to be a double source of authority, on the one hand the written Torah given to Moses on Mount Sinai, on the other the oral Law handed down unwritten over many generations, eventually to be set down in Mishnah and Talmud. Thus for legal derivation—and legal derivation is the essential intellectual/moral core of Judaism, corresponding in this to the place of theology or doctrine in Christianity—the real and effective 'canon' of authority is not the canon of scripture but a 'canon' that is half within scripture and half outside of it: in rough terms, the Torah and the Talmud. Thus even if the 'canon' of scripture was clearly fixed, this was a less important and less decisive fact than would seem natural to those who have seen the notion of the canon through the glass of the Calvinistic Reformation. Some vagueness about the edges and the organization of the canon was tolerable; and this was true in early Christianity also, right up through the first few centuries. In neither case was the canon the determinator of the character of the religion: in so far as this was true, it was true of a portion of the canon, in Judaism the Torah, in Christianity—as Irenaeus saw it—above all the four Gospels, but also St. Paul and Acts.

The New Testament had before it a body of 'holy scriptures' of the Jews. We often say, approximately, that it had 'the Old Testament', but we do not certainly know that its holy scriptures coincided with what we now call by this name. The existence of authoritative holy scripture is beyond doubt, but we do not know exactly what it comprised, or whether it was thought to have precise boundaries at all. The great bulk of quotations in the New Testament comes from the Torah, the Prophets (including Daniel) and the Psalms; in fact, it has been reckoned that practically half of the explicit quotations in the New Testament come from Isaiah and the Psalms put together.[11] In other words, there was a backbone of essential material that was alluded to again and again. The closer we go towards the margin, however, the more difficult it is to be sure: are there quotations of the more marginal books, of

---

[11] Cf. H.B. Swete, *Introduction to the Old Testament in Greek* (Cambridge, 1900), p. 386.

Esther, Song of Songs, Ecclesiastes? If books like these are not cited, it may be that their canonical status was still doubtful,[12] or simply that their content was not felt to be of great value for Christians at the time, or indeed that nobody had bothered in the slightest about the question. The influence of Hellenistic Jewish writings such as Wisdom, not to speak of even remoter apocryphal writings, was surely greater than that of these 'canonical' books;[13] and it is well known that the Book of Enoch is actually quoted (Jude 14–15) with all the appearance of being scripture. Particularly striking is the fact that the powerful analogy of marriage for the relation between Christ and the church is developed in Eph. 5 without any reference to the Song of Songs, something that would hardly have been conceivable in later centuries.[14] Thus the centrality of 'scripture' for the New Testament clearly did not mean that the extent of scripture had to be defined or that attention had to be distributed over it according to its proportions of size and type.

The reason why we cannot be more precise about these questions is, of course, that the New Testament itself was not concerned about them. It contains absolutely no discussion of questions about whether this or that book was canonical. The difference between the Torah and other parts of scripture was obvious, as in all forms of Judaism; and in Christianity the balance between these was altered, some degree of restraint being placed upon the primacy of the Torah and much greater positive emphasis falling upon the Prophets, including Daniel and the Psalms. But nowhere does this lead to any discussion about the way in which the canon is, or should be, organized, or about the balance that ought to obtain between one part and another. Neither do the Christians suggest that

[12] The non-citation of these books could be taken to support the traditional scholarly view that there was still doubt about these books in Judaism until late in the first century AD. It is rather more likely, however, that it provides no evidence for this question, and that the books were simply unimportant for Christianity in New Testament times.

[13] For a useful short summary, see R.H. Pfeiffer in *IDB* i. 512.

[14] The Greek version of the Song, as of Ecclesiastes, has a strongly literalistic translation technique, which may well have been late in the development of ancient biblical translation. We can hardly exclude the possibility that these books did not yet exist in Greek in early New Testament times. This, however, is not of importance for our present question.

the shape of the canon has been distorted through the primacy of the Torah, nor are the Jews represented as objecting to the more determinative role accorded to some of the Prophets. The implication is that the shape of the canon is not in itself considered from either side to be determinative for the selection and interpretation of materials contained in scripture.

Certain peculiar views of the Sadducees, their failure to accept angels, resurrection, and future punishments involving the survival of the soul, are commented on (Acts 23:8, Mt. 22:23), and it is commonly understood that these peculiarities arose from the fact that they would not accept as binding any doctrines not provable from the Torah. But, though these questions are raised in the New Testament, and the contrast between Pharisees and Sadducees is often mentioned, nothing is said that comments on the fact that they depend on different ways of ordering and balancing the canon of scripture. Though Jesus has a profound discussion with a Samaritan woman, and different ideas about the roles of Samaria and Jerusalem in the purpose of God are discussed, nothing is said about the fact that the Samaritan canon is confined to the Torah. Indeed, the reverse is the case, for the woman, by talking of the coming of *Messiah* (John 4:25) suggests the prophetic books rather than the Torah, in which the term *mašiaḥ* in this sense is not used.[15] The fact is, that nowhere in the discussion of any Old Testament passage is the question of its canonical position taken up. It must be considered overwhelmingly evident that questions of the limitation of the canon, the ordering of elements in it, their grouping, and the disputed canonicity of this or that book were simply of no interest to the men of the New Testament.

These considerations are, I suggest, fatal to the notion that the idea of the canon is of first-rate importance for biblical Christianity. Scripture is essential, but canon is not. Canon is a derivative, a secondary or tertiary, concept, of great interest but not of the highest theological importance. It is unlikely in

---

[15] The characteristic Samaritan term corresponding to 'Messiah' is *taheb*, 'the returning one', understood to be based upon the 'prophet like Moses' of Deut. 18:15, 18. It is of course possible that this distinctively Samaritan designation had not yet developed in the first century AD.

face of the biblical evidence that it can be made into the cornerstone of any convincing biblical theology.

To complete this argument, however, we have to look at several further aspects.

It could be argued, first of all, that, even if the men of the New Testament saw it in this way, we in the church of today are bound for theological purposes to the complete scripture, and that means the complete scripture as it stands before us, so that the canonical shape of the whole must be the authoritative structure from which we must work. Theoretically it is a possible argument. We must ask therefore what advantage it could possibly provide. It would seem to lead to one of two things. Either it would force us to read into the minds of the men of the New Testament things that they did not mean. It would lead us to suppose that the writer of 2 Timothy knew exactly the list of books that were in inspired scripture, when he very probably did not; it would lead us to think that Jesus or Paul were highly aware of the status, as canonical or non-canonical, of the books they quoted, when they very likely were not;[16] it would lead us to suppose that the early Christians felt themselves alike under the authority of all the books then canonical, including (say) Esther and Ecclesiastes, and therefore obliged to build them into the structure of Christianity and provide a Christian interpretation of them, when there is no reason to suppose that they were at all interested in the matter. In sum, it would lead us to suppose that scriptural control of the religion was the prime and dominant feature of New Testament Christianity, when in fact it was not. The effect would be a serious and large-scale semantic misreading of a large number of terms in the Greek of the New Testament.

It could be argued, indeed, at least in theory, that we are not men of biblical times. The situation of the men of the Bible, within their own time, could therefore not be fully binding upon us. We have to see scripture as from our position, outside it and long after it. For us therefore it presents itself to us as a complete canon, and not as a

---

[16] I would be more willing to make an exception of St. Paul, because he can be considered more of a 'technical' or 'professional' person with an expert training.

reflection of the historical situation of the men who wrote it. Such a view would be in some accord with certain tendencies of modern hermeneutic thinking. It would be in tune with the rather radical thinking associated with 'cultural relativism'.[17] But those who adhere to the more conservative, scripturally-dominated, thinking of modern canonical criticism would do well to hesitate before espousing it as an argument. As a guide to the church's practice it would be a much more serious breach with traditional Christianity than anything that biblical criticism brought about. It would mean control of interpretation by the needs, real or imagined, of today. One would have to say that, though such and such was St. Paul's meaning, it did not apply to us because we are not biblical men, and that something else was the meaning of the text for today, and therefore was authoritative for us today, although it was not the meaning intended by St. Paul. It is unlikely that those who use this argument will wish to face these consequences. Naturally, there may be biblical texts of a different type, where the 'meaning of the original writer' is more obscure or unattainable, and in some such cases the argument might have some greater force. But St. Paul is also part of the Bible. We cannot use *in general* the argument that we are not biblical men, unless we also accept the implications of it for the interpretation of St. Paul: if we think in this way about other texts, then the reason is some other reason, and not the fact that we are not biblical men. In other words, the argument that we are not biblical men can be followed meaningfully only if we accept the cultural-relativist position, in which case the canon also will be insignificant; it cannot be meaningfully espoused as an argument for a position like recent canonical criticism.

The other possibility would be that scripture would have two meanings: one the meaning as it was for the men of the Bible in their situation, the situation and context of the writing of the books, the other the meaning when all of it is taken together, and separated from all other materials, under the constraint of the canon. This would not be impossible if

[17] On this see my *The Bible in the Modern World* (London: SCM, 1973), pp. 35–52 and *passim*.

both sets of meanings were to be understood as important and as separately discernible, so that one could act as a check upon the other. If one were to say, however, that the canonical meaning must have superior authority and override the meaning of the texts themselves, then one would have a curious sort of mixture, in which some elements were genuinely biblical meanings, in the sense of meanings meant by the biblical writers, others were meanings coming from outside the biblical perspective. This is not such an appalling prospect: on the contrary, it is probably the way in which interpretation has worked most of the time. It would mean, however, that the traditional Protestant appeal to the Bible as supreme source and guide would be very much compromised. In particular, the idea of a biblical mind or a biblical theology, of a biblical point of view as something on the large scale, in spite of qualifications and uncertainties, very different from the church's other traditions and theologies, would become largely inviable. The formation of canons, both in the Old Testament and in the New, was done not only a considerable time after most of the books were written, but under very different theological and intellectual conditions. Athanasius was a great theologian, but he was not by any means a man of the biblical world. In Judaism, between the time when most of the books were written and the time when questions of canonicity came to be discussed, deep and far-reaching changes in the religion and its intellectual structure had taken place. Canonization was done under a faith structure very different from that of the biblical community. For Christianity this means in effect a sharing of authority between scripture and the patristic period: I think that this, rather than the novel fashions of canonical criticism, is the real alternative to the lines that modern biblical scholarship has followed.

It should be observed that none of the above argument depends in any way upon operations of the kind regarded as 'critical'. It does not depend on any of the separation of sources, doubting of historicity, assignment to authors other than those named in the text, or other operations which are commonly supposed to be the meat and drink of critical scholarship. What I have said is, I think, a probable understanding based on the plain sense of the texts as they stand. The conflict, if there is one, is not between a 'critical' judgement and a 'canonical' judgement; rather, it is between the sense of the texts themselves, as perceived whether we are 'critical' or not, and the sense as it is seen when a 'canonical' focus is considered to be normative and the texts are therefore read in the light of it. The evidence of the New Testament in its plain sense is, I think, clear. The problem is the distortion of meanings in the New Testament if one holds that its words must be read as if the importance of the canon were central to their sense. It is perfectly understandable that the theologians of an earlier time did this, if the difference had not been realized. It is something other if we deliberately resolve to do it, once our attention has been attracted to the difference.

We may now proceed to a further point: canons are not particularly hermeneutical in their character. One of the deepest assumptions of modern canonical criticism is that canons give hermeneutical guidance and are intended to do so. This, however, is not their function. The canon does not tell us whether the Synoptic Gospels are to be understood in the light of John, or the reverse, or whether Paul is to be understood in the light of the Gospels or the reverse. Even if a community has a stepped canon, with perhaps prime reverence accorded to the Gospels, this does not necessarily and explicitly rule that St. Paul should be understood in the light of the Gospels: the reverse would still be possible. That is to say, even a stepped canon does not give explicit hermeneutic instructions. Where a law exists in different forms in Leviticus and Deuteronomy, the canon as such does not tell us which should be taken as the dominant. On basic questions concerning the balance of the biblical evidence, such as the question whether justification by faith is the kernel of the Gospel, or whether predestination is rightly considered as an architectonic theme, or whether the idea of creation is theologically derivative from redemption or not, the canon as such seems to tell us nothing.[18] Even where a canonical decision might have some interpretative value, it is often ambiguous. The Book of Revelation was long rejected by

[18] Cf. already *JSOT* 16, 1980, 22.

some areas of the Eastern church, and this opposition to it might well be explained through dislike of chiliasm, Montanism, and the like;[19] but this does not mean that the eventual acceptance of the book signifies an acceptance of the salutary quality of apocalyptic ideas, for that may have had nothing to do with the matter. In so far as such decisions give hermeneutic guidance, that guidance is dependent not on the mere fact of what is or is not within the canon, but on external evidence which may reveal the motives and considerations that came into play

More important, however, for our purpose is the position of the New Testament, and this brings us back to points that have already been made in part. I have already stressed the difference between Jesus and the scribal interpreter.[20] We can now carry this farther and say: the stance of Jesus towards the Old Testament is not primarily an exegetical one. There are indeed a multitude of references to the Old Testament and quotations from it; but Jesus' teaching does not set out to be, and is not, an exegesis. He does not usually start out from scriptural passages and end up with a statement of their meaning. Scripture comes in as an element in the argument, as a powerful illustration and confirmation, as an indication of something that has been left out or overlooked by current religious ideas. 'Well did Isaiah prophesy of you hypocrites, as it is written. . . .' (Mark 7:6): such a saying is not so much an interpretation of Isaiah as an interpretation of the present situation through the use of Isaiah. It is so also with: 'did you never read what David did . . . how he entered the house of God and ate the bread of the presence?' (Mark 2:26). When Jesus uses the 110th Psalm, pointing out that David says, 'The Lord says to my Lord . . . ' (Mark 12:36), Jesus does not arrive at an interpretation of the Psalm but uses it as an enigma: David calls him Lord, how then is he his son? The common people, we are told, heard him gladly; but it is not likely that they went away with a clear idea of what the Psalm actually meant. It was Jesus, not the Psalm, that was being interpreted.

---

[19] On this see Campenhausen, pp. 214ff.
[20] Cf. above, pp. 18f.

By contrast it is the *parable* that is particularly characteristic of Jesus' teaching. The parable stands at the other end of the scale of genres from the interpretation of texts; it begins not from scripture but from an illustration taken from experience of life. Jesus, in presenting and interpreting himself, *could* work from a basis in canonical scripture; but he could work equally well from the imaginative fiction of the parable; and he could work also from uncanonical proverbs and sayings of all kinds. Again, in view of all that has been said in this century to emphasize the *narration of history* as the prime mode of biblical discourse, based on the Old Testament, it is striking that Jesus used historical narration very little.[21]

More generally, all attempts to investigate how the New Testament 'interpreted' the Old run against one difficulty, namely that the New Testament offers 'interpretations' only of limited and scattered portions of the Old, and few of them seen in full context; so that we really have no idea how someone like St. Paul would have proceeded if he had been required to furnish a Christian commentary or interpretation on a full sequential passage, let us say the story of creation (Gen. 1 or 1–3) or the ritual of the red heifer (Num. 19) or the law of the Hebrew slave (e.g. Exod. 21:1–11, Deut. 15:12–18). One is tempted to think that, if we had such an interpretation, it would be much more allegorical in nature than what we find in the New Testament, in other words more like what we find in the Epistle of Barnabas, which does try to tackle exactly that sort of thing. In other words, allegory is restricted in the New Testament because few attempts were made to interpret passages as a whole.[22] Even the exceedingly crude commentary technique of the Qumran *pesher* is hardly to be found in it.

All this is so for a simple reason, namely that the New Testament never set out to be an interpretation of the Old and

---

[21] The genre of rehearsal in summary of the Old Testament story, best known from Stephen's speech in Acts 7, which covers the ground from Abraham down to Solomon before breaking off into accusations of the stiff-necked and persecuting attitudes of the people, is not in fact very common in the New Testament; cf. St. Paul in Acts 13.

[22] On these questions see already my *Old and New in Interpretation*.

did not turn out to be one either. It was a pleasant joke to say
that the New Testament was the first good commentary on
the Bible, but it was never anything more than a joke. Taken
seriously, it was damaging, for it suggested that the relation
between the Old and the New Testaments was basically a
hermeneutic one. Ricoeur exaggerates when he says that 'the
kerygma is the rereading of an ancient scripture': one could
rightly say that the kerygma permits or enables or encourages
the rereading of an ancient scripture, but it is not in essence
such a rereading.[23] The business of the New Testament is not
primarily to tell what the Old really means, but to declare a
new substance which for the Old was not yet there, although
it was understood that it had prophesied its future coming.
The task of the New Testament was not primarily to interpret
the Old, but to interpret that new substance. It is more correct
to say that the Old Testament was used to interpret the
situations and events of the New. In spite of the massive use
of the Old Testament and its networks or meaning, the New
Testament is more like creative literature than like exegesis.

It will be appropriate to conclude this chapter with a brief
survey of one other related question, which has already been
briefly mentioned,[24] namely the idea of a 'canon within the
canon'. Some think that such an inner 'canon' is a good thing,
because it acts as a guide to the centre of the faith and thus to
the interpretation of the remainder of scripture; or, if it is not
a good thing, it is at least a necessary thing. Others think that
it is a bad thing, because it is subjective or otherwise improper
to make any selection, to select any inner 'canon' out of the
whole, and that one must therefore have only the entire canon
as it stands, with no kind of selection of or preference for
elements within it. The discussion of this has been very
confused and it is quite possible that the entire matter is a
non-question. All exegetes and theologians, as we have seen,[25]
organize and structure the material of the text in this or that
way; they cannot work unless they do so. One form of such

[23] P. Ricoeur, *Essays on Biblical Interpretation* (London: SPCK, 1981), p. 51; cf. my
review in *Theology* 84, 1981, 462–4. French original in Ricoeur's preface to R.
Bultmann, *Jésus, mythologie et démythologisation* (Paris: du Seuil, 1968).
[24] Cf. above, p. 41.
[25] Cf. above, pp. 38ff.

organization is to take a preferred stratum, which can be thought to form a vantage-point for the viewing of the whole: let us say, St. Paul's justification by faith, or incarnation as seen by St. John, or perhaps Deuteronomy as centre for the theological understanding of the Old Testament. If such preferences are formed, do they really constitute a 'canon within the canon'? Probably not. A canon, in the sense of the canon of scripture, is: 1. a body of texts; 2. something public, declared authoritative for the whole community; 3. something understood to be permanent and not intended for revision.

If a theologian takes a biblical theme, such as justification by faith, or incarnation, as his primary guide, that is not, or not necessarily, a text; it is not a public canon, but rather his own working guide; and it is not permanent, but is subject to revision on further thought. Moreover, as we have seen, some organizing and structuring of the material has to be done by the theological interpreter in any case. This is not avoided by refusing any statement of priorities and professing to take the entire canon as the sole base. For the canon does not interpret itself. Thus the (Calvinist?) interpreter who takes the whole canon as one entirety but discovers that predestination is the governing theme is not being better guided or more objective than the (Lutheran?) interpreter who says that he is taking St. Paul and justification as his guide from the beginning or the (Anglican?) interpreter who takes St. John as guide. None of these is actually forming an inner 'canon' within the canon. What people call an inner 'canon' is really a principle of theological organization: in other words, when used of the inner 'canon', the word 'canon' is being used metaphorically.

Another way of looking at this is when the inner 'canon' is something extrinsic, extra-textual, e.g. a core of historical events, things that really happened or teachings that were genuinely given. In this case the inner 'canon' is again a metaphor, since it is not a text and is not 'within' the canon at all. It is the external events or thoughts about which the canonical text tells. Selections of key events or thoughts of this kind may be properly criticized because they are wrongly chosen or defined, e.g. on grounds of being historically demonstrable or of being compatible with some non-biblical standard or world-view; but it is not clear that they are liable to valid criticism merely on the grounds that they are references to extrinsic realities.

It is not clear, therefore, that there is any real issue in the debate for and against a 'canon within the canon'. Those who think that such an inner 'canon' exists and is necessary do not usually means a canon at all; those who are against it, and insist that one must work purely from the one canon of scripture as it stands, nevertheless have their own system of priorities and selections. There is no good ground for supposing that reference to extrinsic realities in any way overrules or damages the authority of the canon of scripture. And, one might perhaps say, nothing much is to be gained by supposing that canonicity is the 'canon within the canon'.

If it should, however, be necessary to press the question, and to grant that the idea of a 'canon within the canon' is in some way an appropriate term, then we should ask whether there may not be some important precedents in ancient times. First of all, there is the stepped character of the Jewish Bible, qualified as it is,[26] with the enormous preponderance of the Torah exercising a strong influence on all interpretation of the other parts. As we have seen, however, the canon as such does not specify the greater importance of the Torah: its dominance comes from the religion, which decrees that the Torah is paramount; and, this being given, the stepped nature of the canon testifies to the dominance of the Torah. Secondly, there is the fact we have already noticed, that the New Testament itself made no attempt at a level and balanced account of all parts of the Old, but concentrated its attention on a highly selected set of passages, which formed far from a representative selection from the total Hebrew canon. In a very vague way, it could be said that the New Testament accepted an inner canon within the Old Testament. Thirdly, and more important, there is the creed, the *regula fidei*, for which the Greek word κανών was often used. The church which canonized the scriptures was not a church which supposed for one moment that the scriptures on their own, taken solely after the contours and proportions of the

---

[26] Cf. above, p. 60, where I indicate that the three steps of the Jewish canon do not correspond exactly to grades of religious importance.

canon, would guide correctly to the true shape of the church's faith. Alongside the scripture there was the creed, as the statement of essentials of the faith, which would then be a guide to the interpretation of scripture. Naturally, the existing creeds may or may not be good guides in this respect, but that is not the question. It was only in Protestantism, and in fact only in rather radical currents of it, that it was supposed that the contours of scripture taken for themselves led directly to theological truth. In fact many central currents of Protestantism were strongly confessional, that is, they accepted direction by a Reformational confession that was understood to be derived from scripture and to state the essentials of it; and the creeds of the ancient church were also in large measure accepted. For this argument, however, the ancient creeds are the more correct symbol: they symbolize the fact, not only that the churches have normally accepted the necessity of a confessional statement as guide to the scripture, that is, that they have not relied on the patterns of the biblical canon itself; but, in the case of the ancient creeds, the document is not derived or deduced from scripture, but is supposed to antedate scripture; and whether this is true or not of the creeds that we now know, it rightly symbolizes the essential fact, namely that the faith of the church preceded scripture and generated it, and also accompanied it as its guide and interpreter.

And finally, if we must talk of a 'canon within the canon', in the sense of an inner text lying within a larger text, one might well ask whether for Christianity the New Testament might not be this inner canon, lying within the total compass of the Bible. This would be only another way of saying what has often been said, that the Old Testament, within the church, is known and understood through the mediation of the New.

We suggest, then, that the idea of a 'canon within the canon' is not a very appropriate or exact expression for any major theological option; but, if the term is to be used, reasonably good supports and precedents for such an interior canon can be found. It is the idea of a flat, level, and equal canon that is more difficult to defend on the basis of theological tradition.

One final remark. A notable feature of the modern history of the church has been the stability of the canon. Although small mutterings of unrest have occasionally been heard, practically no attempt to alter the canon of scripture has been made; and this is a very satisfactory position. It is a recognition that the canon, like scripture itself, is the product of a past historical situation in the development of Christianity. The choice between the larger canon of Orthodox and Catholic Christianity and the narrower canon of Protestantism is a choice between two (or, rather, more than two) canons that were in existence more or less at the same time. The existence of this happy agreement, however, depends on one fact: namely, that the church is not too strict in insisting upon the canon as the ultimate measure and standard of what it does and says. If it did so, the results would be an upsurge of very substantial dissatisfaction with the canon, and of proposals to reform it. Paradoxically, the biblicist insistence on a canon composed only of exactly the books which the New Testament church regarded as inspired is the position that would most naturally lead to a demand for reform.[27] The taking relatively easily 'of the canon is a very salutary policy for the church.

[27] In other words, if one were to insist that the actual assertions and beliefs of the New Testament about the boundaries of the canon were to be exactly mandatory upon the church, then, as has been seen, some considerable alteration of the present (Protestant) canon would have to be envisaged.

IV

Further adventures of the canon: 'canon' as the final shape of the text

MODERN canonical criticism, as best represented by Professor Childs, uses the words 'canon' and 'canonical' for three different things, which I shall call canon 1, canon 2, and canon 3. So far we have been talking entirely about canon 1, which is the usual sense of the word 'canon', the list of books which together comprise holy scripture. Canonical criticism maintains that it is essential to scripture that it is a canon, a totality marked off as such, and that the lines and contours formed by the canon and its shape provide the essential guidance to the true meaning.

With canon 2 we come to a different point. Canon 2 is the final form, the so-called 'canonical form', of a book, an individual book, as it stands in the Bible. In many biblical books, as is well known, scholars have identified earlier sources: in Genesis, for example, or in Matthew, who is supposed to have used Mark and another document, common to him and to Luke, known as Q, as well as other materials peculiar to himself. Scholars have been very interested in identifying and studying these earlier, and as some think more 'original', forms of books. In Genesis they have thought they could identify an older story of the beginnings of man (Gen. 2–3; 'J') and a later story (Gen. 1:1–2:4; 'P'), which later came to be combined by an editorial process. Often scholars have thought that the earlier stages, though possibly more obscure, were also more profound and significant. In any case the process of analysing the books in order to identify earlier and later elements has been a main item in the traditional 'introduction'.

Today, however, there is a strong and increasing interest in the final text as against the elements out of which it was formed: the emphasis falls not on the original source, but on that which came out of the editorial process, the work as it stands complete, as the final editors decided to leave it to posterity, the 'canonical' text in that sense. The canonical form is the shape of a book as a whole, as it takes its place within holy scripture. Canon 2 therefore is the final form. It is a little doubtful whether canon 2 should really be called a 'canon' or 'canonical', but the usage has already established itself. We shall have to examine in detail how the emphasis on canon 2 works out; but, to give a simple first indication, it is the view of a canonical critic like Childs that, while it is quite legitimate to look for and identify the earlier stages and sources lying behind a book, this is a quite different operation, or a quite different 'context', from that of approaching it as holy scripture, and that, for theological and church use, only the present, the final, form is relevant.

If canon 2 is the final form of each book, as opposed to earlier stages and sources, what is canon 3? Canon 3 is more a perspective, a way of looking at texts, a perception for which the term 'holistic' is often used. It is through such a holistic stance that the community relates itself to holy scripture and submits itself to its authority. The community is concerned with scripture viewed as a whole and as it stands, and canon 3 is thus a principle of finality and authority. If canonical criticism shows an antipathy towards traditional biblical criticism, it is not so much because of its untraditional results but because of its analytic methods, which seemed to go against the holistic emphasis.[1] Similarly canonical criticism, at least in Childs's version of it, is unsympathetic towards explanations of texts that depend on sociology and on other reconstructions of the world outside the actual theological intention of the text, because these are thought to disturb the holistic vision. Texts are meant to be understood on the basis of the lines of meaning within the totality of the text, and other forms of understanding are not relevant for church life and theology. Canon 3 is not a canon in any ordinary sense of the word, it is rather the principle of attraction, value, and

[1] To illustrate by a contrast, the traditional conservative reaction would be against both the analytic method and its results, but particularly the latter: it would not object to the analytic method if it produced conservative results. Canonical criticism is more troubled by an analytic approach itself. It does not oppose radical results, but objects to the analytic atmosphere in which people embark upon their research.

satisfaction that makes everything about canons and canonicity beautiful.

Now all these kinds of emphasis upon canons, including 1, 2, and 3, have a certain amount of common ground with traditional Christianity, for example with Reformation attitudes, in which the oneness of scripture was stressed. But canon 2, the emphasis upon the final text as distinct from the previously existing sources, has a certain affinity also with modern and quite non-theological ideas about literature. According to many forms of modern literary theory, a literary work has to be understood on its own terms and in the form as it stands before us. Previous sources, stages, and editions, even if they can be discerned, are basically irrelevant. The time and circumstances of composition may not be tremendously important either, and in any case with many works cannot be exactly known. Indeed even the intention of the author may be considered to be irrelevant. A writing as a piece of literary art takes on a meaning of its own. The text becomes sovereign over its own meaning: it creates the 'world of the text' with its own particular structure, its own symbolic coherence and its own capacity to generate communication. Its effect, therefore, is not circumscribed by the circumstances of the author, nor by those of his original audience.

The word 'original', which I have just used, is a good example to illustrate the ethos of canonical criticism. If in traditional biblical criticism the quest for the 'original'—the 'original' text, the 'original' words of Amos, the 'original' form of a parable of Jesus—was a quest for the best possible, in canonical criticism it has become a distinctly bad thing. Nothing is more maddening to the canonical critic than the idea that the original is better or is somehow more desirable or more important. This shift of interest applies in a whole series of departments of biblical study. It applies in textual criticism, where we now hear that we should be interested in the 'canonical text' rather than in the original text; it applies in literary sources, where we are told that we must be interested only in the final form of the parable and not in the way in which Jesus may perhaps have spoken it; and it applies in matters of the religion and theology of the Bible, where we are instructed not to ask what was the actual theology of Amos but what is the theological intention of the canonical book named after him. In other words, a whole series of questions, which biblical scholars have been accustomed to ask, have become wrong questions in the eyes of canonical criticism. One may indeed ask them, as a matter of historical or literary research, but that is a completely different matter from the theological interpretation of scripture and can contribute nothing towards it. For the theological interpretation of scripture one has to begin again at the bottom with the text as it stands and work from the patterns and contours of the final text. Thus if at an earlier stage 'original' was a good word, its status in that respect has now been taken over by its opposite, 'final'. In these respects canonical criticism supports itself upon a dual foundation: on the one hand theological convictions, and ideas built up from the experience of exegesis, on the other hand more general cultural and literary trends. While some presentations of canonical criticism lay more stress on the former, the appeal of the movement and its favourable reception certainly owe a great deal to the latter. The whole movement in literary study from historical explanation to study of a text as a synchronic entity, meaningful in its own right, forms the background against which canonical criticism may flourish.[2]

Now from the point of view of canonical criticism all these three things, canon 1, canon 2, and canon 3, belong together. Actually, as will be shown, they are very different and at times conflict. The strategy of canonical criticism lumps them together, because it is thought that all three have alike been neglected in scholarship, and this gives a unitary character to a scholarly programme which demands more attention to all three. Because all three are regarded as good things, canonical criticism has not troubled to notice that they function in very

---

[2] Particularly in Childs's version, canonical criticism is rather sharply differentiated from literary understanding, and the emphasis is placed upon the theological role, as a text possessing divine authority for the community: see his *Introduction*, p. 74, and also his sharp (if ill-argued) rejection of the approach of Paul Ricoeur through the metaphoric and symbolic power of scripture, ibid., p. 77. In spite of this dissociation from the literary approach, it remains highly probable that these literary insights, which have deservedly raised considerable interest among biblical scholars, are a major source of the appeal and interest which canonical criticism has gained. See below, pp. 158ff.

different ways; this is so much so that it is very misleading to designate them all by the same word 'canon' in the first place. Part of the attractiveness of the term 'canon' is that it seems to be an objective term, in the sense that all scholars know that there is a canon of scripture and that scripture in this sense is a closed corpus, bounded by the canon; scholars may differ about the history and character of the canon, but the existence of it is agreed (though, as we have seen, this is true only if we take our stand within the post-New Testament world); but this objectivity of the canon applies only to canon 1. It is a fact about scripture that it has a canon. But canon 3, the holistic emphasis, is not a fact in this sense, it is a value judgement; and even if scripture is or has a canon in the sense of canon 1 this in itself does not prove that the value judgement of canon 3 is valid or necessary. Conversely, even if it can be shown that canon 3 is true and that the community views and accepts the Bible 'holistically', it does not follow that this buttresses the importance or centrality of canon 1, since a holistic view of scripture is perfectly possible without paying much attention to canon 1. Again, canon 2, the final form of each individual book, is in a way an objective fact, in that there is no doubt about the existence of such a final form; but the question about the authority of that final form for the interpretation of that individual book is quite independent of canon 1, the canon of scripture as a whole, and of canon 3, the holistic vision. By using the one word 'canon' for all three it is made to seem as if the valuations of canons 2 and 3 are rightly entailed by the factual and objective character of canon 1. But when one shows that canon 1, though a factual reality, is not as dominant in scripture as it has seemed, one is told that this results from failure to see the new and wider sense of 'canon'.[3] In other words, at this point canonical criticism depends upon systematic confusion in the use of its favourite word, 'canon'. Actually, it would have been more candid and more correct to restrict 'canon' to canon 1; but it is not likely that this will now be done.

These are not purely theoretical distinctions, but can be

---

[3] Cf. Childs in *JSOT* 16, 1980, 53: 'Some of the misunderstanding of parts of my book stem from replacing my broad use of the term with a much narrower, traditional usage, and thus missing the force of the argument.'

shown to have applied in the actual dynamics of the creation of scripture. Most important in this regard is the difference of character between canon 1 and canon 2, between the canon of scripture as the list of books and the final form of an individual book as distinct from sources and previous forms. The processes by which the two are reached seem to be quite different. One is a theological and/or ritual decision that concerns the weight and the authority to be given to a book; the other is a literary process, part of the production of the book itself. More important still, the two are not only different, I suggest that in the case at least of the Old Testament they were often contradictory. The feeling for literary genre and its relation to meaning, which goes along with the full form of a book at any stage of its formation, was still alive in the literary redaction of the books, but the process of canonization, far from preserving that feeling, did much to destroy it. Canonization as holy scripture, given the ideas of inspiration that both Judaism and, later, Christianity then held, led not to the heightened appreciation of literary genres but to the loss of that appreciation; it led not to the high evaluation of the shape of books as a whole but to the neglect of it. For, as these ideas of inspiration operated, books came to be seen as inspired not only, and not even primarily, as complete wholes: they were inspired also in every individual part, and in extreme cases down even to sub-semantic segments. Thus, both in traditional Judaism and in traditional Christianity, law or doctrine could be proved from individual scripture passages without anyone worrying in the slightest that these passages, if read in the light of their actual literary genre and total shape as a literary work, did not mean at all what people understood them to mean. This is not to say that the total meaning of the books, according to their genre, was left unknown; this depended on what the individual book was like. But, in addition to the general meanings of the whole, scripture was allowed, and encouraged, to function through its parts. The vision of all scripture as one whole reduced the individuality of the various books. Midrashic exegesis in Judaism was a good example. One of its chief mechanisms was that whereby a linguistic item, occurring in a particular context, can be read with the senses appropriate to that item in other contexts. In other words, it works by means of a massive decontextualization. It relied to a high degree upon the canon, in that the scriptural canon was the field from which many of the senses were selected—though this was not universal, for senses could be drawn simply from colloquial Aramaic or Hebrew usage, independently of source—but the canon did not fix the context, it provided freedom from the constraints of context. What controlled midrashic exegesis was not the canon, but the religion, in this case Judaism as it had become. In Christianity the demonstration of doctrine by proof-texts followed a similar pattern. The vision of the whole which was possessed by the reader was derived not from the canon of scripture, but from the dictates of the religion.

Thus, for example, the Qumran community, interpreting the book of Habakkuk, did not for a moment think about the canonical shape of this book as a guide to genre and thereby to meaning. Their principle was a quite different one. All scripture was about them themselves, their own community and its various crises and vicissitudes. Each phrase, therefore, could be related directly to things that were happening, or had just happened, in the experience of their community. Much early Christian interpretation was like this too.[4]

It may perhaps be claimed for Reformational exegesis that it did much to recover for Christianity a full sense of the relation between genre and meaning in books. Perhaps this is too much to claim, but there is something in it. In so far as there is something in it, it was not so much because of the theological innovations of the Reformation as because it was related to the whole literary revival of the Renaissance, with its appreciation of the ancient classics and the way in which they should be read, a sort of reading quite different from that of the mediaeval schoolmen. Calvin himself had been something of a classical scholar and had written a commentary on Seneca's *De Clementia* (1532). His commentaries had a considerable grasp of style and genre. This could lead, as a grasp of style and genre must lead, in a *critical* direction: it was on stylistic grounds that Calvin seriously doubted whether Peter could have written 2 Peter. His beliefs about

[4] See below, p. 97f.

scripture made it difficult for him to follow his stylistic insights in this: what is striking is that these insights were strong enough for him to form these doubts in the first place at all.[5]

In this respect, however, the practice of the New Testament in its reference to the Old was quite different. Passages were quoted and used in relation to their context and genre and they were also quoted and used quite independently of their context and genre.[6] To take up again an instance already referred to above,[7] the use by Jesus of 'I said: you are gods' in John 10:34 cannot easily be justified from the canonical shape of Ps. 82, which makes it plain that the reference is not to men hearing the Word of God, but to gods, and gods other than the God of Israel, and that these gods are about to suffer disaster. Nor can it be justified by the total canon of the Hebrew Bible which, as Jews have always seen, makes it highly unlikely that human beings would be seriously depicted as 'gods'. As John sees it, on the other hand, Jesus is in fact Son of God, and there is to be found in scripture a passage containing words which express this fact; it is a passage which fits into the situation of Jesus and his contemporaries, and it is this setting in the life of Jesus, not the canonical form within the Hebrew Bible, that determines his use of it. For any kind of strictly *canonical* principle of exegesis the interrelation of Old and New Testaments must be of great importance, and if the New Testament failed to see things 'canonically' that must be a serious objection to any attempt to maintain that the canon is central.

With this we may, however, pass on to another stage of the discussion. The previous chapter maintained that the New Testament showed little or no interest in questions of the canonicity of the Old Testament books (here the reference is to canon 1, the canon of scripture). This may well have prompted the question: granted that the men of the New

---

[5] On the other hand one must take into account the fact that 2 Peter was already questioned in the ancient church on grounds of style, as my wife points out to me: would Calvin have been so sensitive to the stylistic question if he had not known this?

[6] Cf. my *Old and New in Interpretation*, pp. 142 f., where I conclude that 'interpretation was generally done as if true results could be obtained whether context was noticed or not'.

[7] Cf. above, p. 17.

Testament were not interested in the final arrangements of the canon, in the question whether Esther and Ecclesiastes were in or whether Enoch and Wisdom were out, or in what way the canon was balanced and arranged, and granted that there was still perhaps no final canon of scripture at all, may it not be perhaps that the principle of a canon was already there? Was there not, back into early Old Testament times, a sort of core of central and agreed tradition, a body of writings already recognized and revered, which—even if it was not a canon—functioned in relation to the community of the time in the same general way in which the canon of scripture functioned for later generations? Was there not a sort of 'pre-scripture' or 'pre-canon', traces of which can be seen within the Old Testament itself, and still more in the intertestamental writings and Ben Sira? Was there not indeed some such pre-canon as far back as the time of David and Solomon? Could one not in this sense argue that the whole nature of Israelite religion was canonical, that it depended on the selection of a limited set of traditions which were accepted and were to be authoritative in the community? Was not this pre-scripture or pre-canon the forerunner of the scripture which was eventually to emerge, to be defined still later by its canon? I would myself very much affirm just these things. But observe the consequences if we do so. We do not have the pre-canon, and we cannot have access to it except through historical reconstruction. Only a critical reconstruction can tell us what was in the pre-canon in the time of Solomon or of Isaiah. The importance of the pre-canon, if it is granted, is a strong reason for the importance of source criticism in the Pentateuch or for the dating of the various prophetic passages and other such critical procedures. If we are to follow this line, the prototype canonical critic is not Childs but Wellhausen. For it was Wellhausen and those like him who were interested in telling us, though they did not use these words, just what was in the pre-canon in the days of Solomon and Isaiah. Modern canonical criticism has claimed also that it links the biblical texts with the community in which they were used. But this is exactly true of Wellhausen, and indeed was the essential of his approach to the identification and dating of the sources. Institutions of the community like the priesthood, the laws concerning homicide, the regulations about the altar or about tithes or about slave release, could be located within a historical sequence of the community's life; and the sequence thus seen in that community's life provided the sequence for the documentary sources and thus the means by which the contents and dimensions of the pre-canon could be identified. Of course Wellhausen may have been quite wrong in his conclusions; but, if we are to build upon the idea of a continuing and growing pre-canon throughout Israel's history, Wellhausen is one who has shown us very well how it can be done. The most important point, however, is this: all interest in a pre-canon must necessarily mean the abandonment of the idea that interest in a canon means interest in *finality*, concentration on the final stage of the canon as against earlier stages. In other words, if canon 1 is to be saved from shipwreck through appeal to the pre-canon, canon 2 has to be thrown overboard. That analysis of books, which takes departure from their final canonical form and proceeds to discover earlier and datable sources, is canonically justified by the need to recognize and evaluate the pre-canon.

There are several further ways in which this should be followed up. As we have seen, modern canonical criticism has reacted, often violently, against the idea that the 'original' is the most important datum point for the understanding of texts. And I have at various times said this myself, that the concentration on the original needs to be complemented by an equal interest in the effects and the after-history of a text. But one must also ask whether the tradition of scholarship did not after all have some sort of good reasons for the line it took: for scholars were not all foolish or incompetent. Even if they expressed badly the values they attached to the 'original', or—as was more often the case— did not express them at all, it may be that the term implied some indispensable part of working method. We can see this, first of all, in the case of textual criticism, one of the areas in which the use of the term 'original' is most obvious.[8] It is certainly mistaken to suppose that textual criticism works by seeking to recover the original

[8] It is also one of the first areas in which in his *Introduction* Childs develops his contrast between the original and the final, see his pp. 88–99.

copy or autograph.[9] The 'original' in so absolute a sense is not necessarily very important. In actual textual criticism 'original' functions in a somewhat different way, for it is used relatively: given the fact of different readings, a normal and probably a necessary way of ordering, classifying, and understanding them is to ask which of them may probably be considered secondary and derivative in relation to others; and what is thus perceived to be not secondary and derivative in relation to other readings is in that respect more 'original'. It is doubtful whether any serious thinking about the text at all can be carried out without this piece of conceptual apparatus.

Secondly, there is the question of the meaning of words. What do the words of the Bible mean, on the simplest level of lexical, semantic identity? Many modern studies have emphasized that a word, a lexical unit, means something only as a functioning unit within the synchronic language system of a certain time. This emphasis on the synchronic, as against the diachronic axis with its interest in the change and derivation of languages and linguistic elements in time, has suggested to some the implication that the Bible should be read synchronically, as a unity existing at one time. And it may well be that some important progress can be made along that line. But surely the synchronic principle works also in the other direction: the words of (say) the prophet Amos must mean what they meant in the language system of the time of Amos, the words of a commentator or glossator three centuries later must be understood as they functioned in the language of his time. In other words, the idea of a synchronic vision, far from inviting the non-historical reading of the Bible, can also be understood as a strong argument in favour of the distinguishing of sources along a temporal axis. The surface meaning of the biblical text disclosing, as it does, only partial lineaments of meaning and being criss-crossed by substantial elements of inconcinnity and contradiction, the scholar is led to discern within the corpus a series of temporally successive strata each of which shows a much higher degree of synchronic identity

---

[9] Childs, ibid., p. 93, quoting from Ralph Klein. Childs has here brought together a number of weak and doubtful *statements* about the nature and purpose of textual work. It is doubtful, however, whether these weaknesses reveal much about the inner structure and logic of textual criticism as generally carried on.

and meaningfulness. In other words, ideas that are broadly structuralist can perfectly well provide the basis for traditional historical criticism, and important elements of the work of traditional critics like Wellhausen can be accounted for in this way.[10] This should not be surprising; after all, biblical criticism arose precisely because people had read the Bible 'canonically' and under the guidance of its surface shape, and this led them in due course to critical observations.

Consider, for instance, the position of the lexicographer of biblical Hebrew or Greek, or the expectations of the user of the dictionary. One could certainly conceive of a dictionary that explained a Hebrew word not only as Jeremiah used it but as it would have been understood in the Maccabaean period, that gave the sense of a New Testament word not only as the author of Matthew had meant it but also as Origen later explained it. Yet it is doubtful whether this is practical as a method of working. The user of the dictionary, doubtless ignorant of synchrony and diachrony, is well led by his instinct when he says to himself: 'What I want is the original meaning'. For it is the original meaning, in the sense of the meaning involved in the construction of the text, that provides something to operate with. The will to know how it was later understood is a perfectly proper scholarly pursuit: but it can only lead in the direction of the historical thesaurus of the post-biblical usage of the languages. What cannot, I think, be done is to set up an arbitrary point, such as the text of the period of the canonization, or the Masoretic period,[11] as a standard. Or, if necessary, one simply has to take more than one stage of meaning and build these together into one's

[10] For some experiments in this direction see R.M. Polzin, *Biblical Structuralism* (*Semeia* Supplements; Fortress Press, Philadelphia and Scholars Press, Missoula, Montana, 1977), pp. 126–201, on Wellhausen, von Rad, and Noth—not to be taken without reserve, but still a pointer in a correct direction.

[11] Cf. J.F.A. Sawyer, *Semantics in Biblical Research* (London: SCM, 1972), which in its principles seems to me to display this arbitrariness. The choice of the Masoretic stage as the base for interpretation seems to depend, in any case, on the misjudgement that supposes Masoretic work to be basically interpretative in character, which seems to me not to be the case. The Masoretes were concerned primarily with the *correct writing* of the text, and only a small proportion of their notes are hermeneutically or exegetically oriented. It is quite unjustified (Sawyer, p. 14) to suppose that the Masoretes 'saw their task as one of handing down a meaningful text'.

understanding: thus it may very well be that 'Son of Man' as spoken by Jesus had a substantially different sense from 'Son of Man' as intended and understood by St. Stephen or St. John. If this is so, then we have two stages each of which is in a sense 'original'; both have to be traced and studied, and worked into our theological understanding. No sense is made by insisting that only the final stage, that of (say) St. John, is canonical and therefore only it is theologically relevant. What Jesus says is part of canonical scripture, if we must put it in this way, as much as the Gospel of St. John in its final form. On the level of the meanings of words, and the operation of grammar, it is difficult to take other than a historical position. It is important, however, to see the sense of 'historical' in the correct way. I mean 'historical' in the sense of focused upon the actual text of scripture at the point, or the various points, of its coming to be. 'Historical' when used of language has often meant a stress on the pre-history of the language, on derivations and etymologies, which even when correct can be semantically misleading. A concentration on the language of the Bible, from the point of view of precision in the understanding of the meanings and grammatical functions, can lead only into a historical direction: in other words, on this level the structural and hermeneutical on the one side, and the historical on the other, do not diverge but support one another. This has not been seen by many canonical critics, whose background lies in such studies as form criticism and religious hermeneutics: whatever directions one is led into on that plane, the plane of language is inclined in another. The various strata of biblical interpretation are not symmorphous: this is why there is no one overriding principle which governs them all in the same way.

It is possible, theoretically, to go in another direction and to say that the meaning of words, as rooted in the usage of the writer, is not final, and that one may take as one's reference point some other understanding of these words. It can be done but it is not, perhaps, as profitable as it seems. What it seems to lead towards is not—if one is honest—a richer or more powerful meaning, but a sort of semantic lacuna. Suppose one has a text with a hole in it, a physical hole, one cannot make precise judgements about the meaning of what was in that hole. All one can make is rather uncertain extrapolations from that which is visible and readable. If this happens with a physical hole in the text, there can also be a semantic hole: signs and words are there, but they cannot be securely read or understood.

Let us take two examples. At 1 Samuel 14:41, something has gone wrong with the army of Israel; the reader knows, though the king and his men do not yet know, that Jonathan unwittingly broke a vow imposed upon Israel by his father; he had eaten some wild honey. So something has to be done to discover the cause of divine anger. The King James version reads:

> Therefore Saul said unto the Lord God of Israel, Give a perfect *lot*.

(The printing of *lot* in italics is a sign that there is no word *lot* here in the Hebrew at all; it is supplied as an explanatory gloss, but all the text really has is something like 'Give perfect', and no more grammatical in Hebrew than it is in English.)

Contrast with this another text, easily accessible to us in the RSV:

> Therefore Saul said, 'O Lord God of Israel, why hast thou not answered thy servant this day? If this guilt is in me or in Jonathan my son, O Lord, God of Israel, give Urim; but if this guilt is in thy people Israel, give Thummim.'

Now the RSV has this much longer text because it has followed the LXX here; and in Samuel scholars have long thought that the LXX at certain places had a text much superior to the Masoretic, and this has now been corroborated by the finds at Qumran of actual Hebrew texts which agree with the LXX against the MT, making it clear that the LXX does not rest on fancy or imagination but on an actual Hebrew basis, now lost apart from fragments.

The difference is that the Greek text here is a fine text, which makes good sense of the entire passage; it explains well the context, it brings to the fore the casting of the two lots, the negative lot Urim and the positive lot Thummim, and it gives a speech by Saul that is entirely in the style and spirit of the rest of the passage. Out of the rather meaningless word 'perfect' of the MT it gives us a clear and apposite reference, not *tamim* 'perfect' but Thummim, a word spelt with the same consonants and, as a noun, fitting well as object after the verb 'give'. There is no real doubt that the Greek text here is substantially the true text; or, perhaps, better, there is no real doubt that the MT is the product of mere error by missing out a piece of text.

Now it is still possible, if one wishes it strongly enough, to continue to take the MT here as the basis for interpretation: it is the canonical text to which the community was attached. But if one does so, then the consequences are to create, or to accept the existence of, a semantic lacuna. One is preferring no sense, or little sense, to good sense. One will have to say simply that there are some words in the text that provide no basis for statements about meaning.

For, we must perceive, the process that, in a case like this, leads to the canonical text is not a hermeneutical one. No one supposed that they were 'interpreting' 1 Samuel 14:41 by leaving out this important piece of text. The omission was fortuitous. Once the piece of text had been lost, of course, something had to be done, the signs had to be made at least pronounceable, and meanings of a kind had to be applied; but these meanings are meanings read into that which is intrinsically lacking in meaning. They are the semi-meanings of the interpreter, not the meanings of the text.

Here is a case of another sort, but with similar implications. At Deut. 33:2 the poem begins with the vision of the Lord coming from Sinai; he appears from Mount Paran, he comes from the ten thousands of his holy ones. The next clause begins 'from his right hand' and ends 'for them (for him?)'; between these there stands the word, or two words, *'eš dat*. The King James Version had 'fiery law': 'from his right hand *went* a fiery law for them'. This is an old understanding; the Vulgate, for instance, had *lex ignea*, a 'fiery law', just the same thing. This depends on taking the first syllable as *'eš* 'fire', which is of course a common Hebrew word in any period. But *dat* cannot be a word for 'law' in the Hebrew of Deuteronomy. Though it exists in Hebrew, and is found in late books like Esther, it is a word of Persian origin, and even when it does enter biblical usage it does not mean 'law' in a sense comparable with the Jewish Torah. In later Hebrew it means 'religion'. Still more, the order of the elements, *'eš* 'fire' followed by *dat*, is not one that can be counted possible as biblical Hebrew in the sense 'fiery law'. The fact is that, if we accept this text as correct, we can only read it by putting ourselves outside the language system of biblical Hebrew. Meaning can be ascribed to the elements, but the meaning is ascribed by ignoring the lexical and grammatical character of the material. Here once again the reading of the traditional text is the recognition of a semantic lacuna: it means that the text has a gap in it, as surely as if there was a physical hole in it. In such a case the resort to textual emendation, or to the search for a meaning, previously unknown in Hebrew but discoverable from another Semitic language, is actually less speculative than the retention of the text. Perhaps such a scholarly search will lead nowhere; and if that is so we will have a semantic lacuna in any case. But the way in which the traditional text may have been read by the late community, the redactors and canonizers, is probably simply not a meaning viable within the language of the text. It is the synchronic understanding of Hebrew as a language that makes the maintenance of a certain historical perspective necessary.

The contrast between the original and the final leads on to a point of a different kind, that lies within the nature and structure of biblical religion. As against the often painful origin-seeking of modern scholarship, canonical criticism has been emphasizing the final stages of the text, its late development, its final form. This is richly ironic, because the Bible itself, read simply as canonical document, goes quite in the opposite direction. It heavily stresses the role of the originator. The founder or proclaimer of a new turn in religion is very prominent in it. Just taking the Bible as it stands, how obviously it stresses the persons who stand at the beginnings of great departures: Moses, Elijah, Amos, John the Baptist, Jesus! Taken as it stands and read by its canonical form, the Bible hardly gives the impression that eighth-century scribes were to be compared in importance with Moses, or that the later disciples of the school of Paul were very considerable figures. The late redactors, the canonizers, the community whose final interpretation passed on scripture to later generations, find scarcely any mention or notice in scripture itself. It may well be that the Bible as it stands is a wrong indication of the facts here, and that Mosaic tradition is as important as Moses, or more important, interpretative tradition as important as the teaching of Jesus himself, if the latter can be discovered. That is the position that much critical opinion seems to have reached; it is odd that the new trends of 'canonical' interpretation at this point so emphasize that critical interest in redaction and in tradents, so little follow the contours of the canon itself. The canonical picture is one that puts the originators in the limelight: it is the books of Moses, the books of the original prophets whose names they bear, that we have before us. It is the great literature of Judaism, like the Mishnah and the Talmud, that shows us a literature that is really concerned to emphasize the process of transmission, the trend to redaction and conclusion: very little of the Bible goes that way. Scripture itself is orientated towards the originators; Islam followed Judaism and Christianity in this. Paradoxically, if 'liberal' criticism, as we see it now, emphasized too strongly the figure of the original genius, the founder who inaugurated the new trends in religion, it was not, perhaps, because it was too critical towards the canonical picture, but because it followed its suggestions too blindly. The emphasis on the crucial role of the originators seems to be built into the canonical picture of the rise of our religion.

There are two points of a more practical nature that follow from these considerations. The first is, perhaps, not very important, but it has significance. The church has always read the Bible in pericopes. One can indeed and should read the Bible as a whole but for purposes of worship, liturgy and preaching rather limited passages have been used since ancient times. It is not possible as a practical procedure to be reading the whole Bible or the whole canon at one time; and I doubt whether there was ever any lectionary system which succeeded in reading *all* the Bible, even over several years. It has been considered normal and right for the church's operation with the Bible in worship to be concerned with pericopes. Now is this not an unfortunate separation of passages from their context? How could one read in worship the story of creation from Gen. 1 without going on to read the story of Eden and the Fall from 2 and 3? Obviously the church has always wanted the context, in the sense of preceding and following passages, to be kept in mind. But how could it agree to a reading in pericopes at all? The assumption has been, I think, and still is, that the individual passage can be read and can be preached upon because of the invisible framework of doctrine that undergirds both of these activities. Awareness of the rest of the Bible must, of course, be there; but it is a mistake to suppose that it is this awareness of the rest *of the Bible* that is the primary factor in justifying the liturgical use of the pericope. It is not the rest of the Bible, but the doctrinal framework, that is the major factor.

More important still, perhaps, is a practical implication for the preacher. Many of the parables of Jesus, for instance, or other pieces of his teaching, appear to have attached to them appendixes or additions which modify or alter the meaning of that which has gone before. Should a preacher or other expositor take as his basis what was probably the earlier text, or must he take the whole thing as one piece, because it is the final text? Is it right for him to mention that the additional pieces were probably not spoken by Jesus himself and represent a modification or a later interpretation, or does he have to suppress such ideas and deal with the whole as if it was one unitary piece? This is the chief practical danger that the rise of canonical criticism has brought about: it has been quick to produce a strong zealotic legalism of the final text, that insists: you *must must must* work from the final form of the text. I think this is completely wrong, and that the preacher is perfectly free to work with a portion representing an earlier stage of the text. He is free to expound the creation story of Genesis 1 without tying it by links of meaning to the quite different story of chapter 2; he is free to expound the pericopes that represent Amos's original message without being forced to integrate them with the quite different message of the book's conclusion; and so similarly for the Book of Job, or for Zechariah, or for Second Isaiah. This is not because what is early and original is authentic and therefore authoritative. What is earlier *was* the text at one time, it was thus 'canonical', if we must call it so, in the biblical period itself. The portion which represents the 'earlier' text is still a legitimate and meaningful pericope of holy scripture. What the Yahwist meant in Gen. 2 is a valid and proper meaning of scripture, and so is what P meant in Gen. 1.[12] We may perhaps group these sections in different ways, and then we would have a succession of somewhat differing meanings, but all of them will be valid and proper meanings of scripture. There is no reason to suppose that the product of final redaction is in any way more valid or more proper. It is important to the community that it should know that a certain portion of text was not in fact part of the teaching of Amos or of Jesus, and the community will attach a wrong meaning to the passages if it is not told of this. Naturally, it is often hard to be certain of these things; but certainty is not so essential. The essential is to know that there is a question about it, that it is at least possible, perhaps likely, that such and such a sentence was not spoken by that person.

Thus the earlier text is not, because it is earlier, automatically superior to the later; but the later, just because it was final, is certainly not superior to the earlier. On the contrary, if we take the main central material as our basis, in either Old or New Testament, it is difficult to doubt that the approach of completeness is signalized by a certain deterioration, by a failure to understand what the basic insights of the contents of the traditions were, by a tendency to compromise on the one side and to harden into rigid systems on the other. This can sometimes be seen in the latest touches added to books, sometimes in the more marginal books added latest to the canon. Who will suppose, for instance, that 2 Peter really understood Christianity as well as 1 Peter, or that the letters to Timothy are in theological content comparable with Romans or Galatians? Of course these are theological judgements, but they are judgements well substantiable precisely through theological discussion. One of the reasons why scripture was fixed as such, and separated from other continuing tradition, was, very likely, the sense that tradition was

---

[12] Cf. McEvenue in *Interpretation* 35, 1981, 238.

deteriorating;[13] and inside the boundaries of scripture the signs of this are not hard to read. To make the community of the canonizing period into the ultimate arbiters of scripture is therefore a dubious step.

We may continue this argument with another aspect of the same problem. Canonical criticism, in at least some of its forms, can be seen as implying an attempt to expel all influence of the history of religion from biblical interpretation. There is scripture itself, and there is theology; theological interpretation is done direct from scripture, and there is no intermediary, since any intermediary would break down the sole dependence on the canonical form of scripture, which alone is authoritative for theology. Other disciplines are purely ancillary at most and tend to be harmful if not carefully restrained. The canon provides all the necessary continuity, not only forward to the post-biblical community but also back to the older community from which the writings came.

The mistake in this seems to be that it implies a continuity on the level of scripture alone. The faith of Israel developed through two channels (perhaps more than two, but at least these two): 1. traditions and scripture; 2. the religion of Israel. These interacted upon one another but they are not in harmony or congruence. Thus, for example, to use a case I have cited before:[14] it is quite possible, as Childs suggests, that the material of Deutero-Isaiah was detached from its original historical context and raised to a general and metaphorical level.[15] It does not follow, however, that this was done through the attachment of Deutero-Isaiah to First Isaiah and it very possibly had nothing to do with that attachment; for, in so far

[13] In the case of the Old Testament one must guard oneself against the notion that Judaism as such represents a deterioration vis-à-vis the Old Testament; but the proper avoidance of this danger should not lead us into closing our eyes to the possible presence of deterioration, as measured by the standards of the major central strata.

[14] *JSOT* 16, 1980, 17, 19; earlier discussion, *Explorations in Theology* 7, p. 46.

[15] Bruce Birch is right, however (*Horizons in Biblical Theology*, 2, 1980, 121), in his careful argument that Childs's 'scattered vestiges' greatly understates the degree to which the Babylonian historical context has been maintained in Deutero-Isaiah. I now feel I was initially much too easily persuaded by parts of Childs's argument. Childs himself has now accepted some correction in this respect; see *Horizons in Biblical Theology* 2, 1980, 205.

as this transformation took place, it was probably applied also to First Isaiah and indeed to much of the biblical material. It had nothing to do with the canonical form of individual books but was a general religious and interpretative change: it was a shift in the religion.

The scriptures might stay as they were, but the religious structure within which life was seen might change. The scriptures might change, but the overall religious structure stay the same. Precisely because most of the material of scripture was ancient material inherited from a much earlier time, it had a sort of inertia which made it resistant to change even when important shifts of attitude took place. This is a reason against exaggerating the viewpoint, rather popular today, that emphasizes that scripture contains always interpretations rather than authentic ancient material. This is all right in theory; but much of the material was resistant to interpretative adjustments; they were just too difficult to make. A great deal of material was retained, I believe, not because later redactors were able to make changes which would shift its significance into line with their own theological positions and interests, but for the opposite reason, that no one could account for its peculiarities or undertake to edit it into the lineaments of modern ideas, and so, being already holy tradition, it was left as it was. Thus the canonical text of scripture is not a faithful index of the religious changes which affected its own development, and conversely the religion of any particular time is not exactly reflected in the scripture. And, most important of all, as already stated, the essential hermeneutical guides, which determined the modes in which scripture might be understood, did not lie within the canon at all but outside it, in the religion.[16]

Take this as an example:[17] when we ask about the tendencies that emerged in later Judaism, such as apocalyptic, we may consider how these related to different ways of relating and balancing the different parts of the older canonical materials: the Torah, the historical books or Former Prophets (though not so called at that time), the

---

[16] See above, p. 67.
[17] In all this section I am deeply indebted to a paper, not yet published, read to a seminar in Oxford by my colleague Dr. John Barton.

Prophets. That is to say, we also can do a piece of canonical criticism; nothing, after all, could be more fascinating. We may perhaps distinguish at least four ways, traceable in the post-biblical literature, in which this material might be weighted and reckoned. Given the fact of the Torah, the question is how the Prophets should then be read and in what direction the line might then be produced beyond them.

The first answer is to read the Prophets as a sort of theological commentary on the Torah. Seen this way, both the narrative materials (the 'Former Prophets') and the prophetic books provide illustrations of the eternal character of God. The material we call historical presents stories which show what God is like. On the surface these are historical, for they narrate things which happened in the past and are constitutive of the present; but this does not matter very much, because the things that happen can often happen again and again: good is rewarded, evil brings disaster. The stories are important, not so much for their narrative movement, as for their paradigmatic quality.[18]

A second answer would be to read the Prophets as a more haggadic or halachic commentary on the Torah and hence, like the Torah itself, a guide to how to live well as a Jew. In the Prophets this mode of reading notes the moral tales in the historical books, such as Nathan's encounter with David, and the moral stringencies of the prophetic writings. The Prophets might then be seen as something like what was later called a 'fence about the Law'.

A third possibility is to see the material as a sort of history, in this sense allowing the historical books or Former Prophets to dominate the picture of the whole. The whole is therefore a story, a story about the past but carrying future elements and implications. Thus the Former Prophets tell how it had been in the past, but they also contain future-predictive elements which show in what direction the past is going; the Latter Prophets also tell of the past, for the major books like Isaiah and Jeremiah have large narrative sections, but they contain even larger future-predictive elements. Such a relation of past

---

[18] On this cf. my *Explorations in Theology 7: the Scope and Authority of the Bible* (London: SCM Press, 1980), p. 36.

and future is not necessarily an 'eschatology', for it does not necessarily have any sense of urgency: rather, God will continue to control things in the future as he has done in the past.

A fourth possibility is to lay the primary emphasis on the predictive material of the Latter Prophets, which prediction is to be seen as an element also within the Former, especially in the two great cases, Nathan's dynastic promise to David (2 Sam. 7) and the words of the man of God from Judah, which named Josiah as the future king who would defile the altar at Bethel (1 Kings 13:2, 2 Kings 23:15–18). The key to all this material, under this mode of reading, is that the end is near and that one's own community is the one that is to be affected. The sense of the predictions had been partly or wholly hidden; but as soon as one realizes that it all applied to one's own group one can understand them.

Each of these approaches can be seen, perhaps, as generating its own kind of literature in the late biblical and post-biblical period. That period was not fruitful in the creation of new genres, not until the arrival of Mishnah and Midrash: many works can better be considered as imitations, as pastiche, based upon older and existing genres. Tales like Esther or Tobit are imitated from the older historical narratives; wisdom writing takes Proverbs as its pattern; post-biblical psalms followed the biblical poems. The post-biblical writings were thus attempts to respond, in roughly the same genres, to the older books when read in a particular way. The way that was preferred depended on the line of development of the religion that was being followed.

The first mode of reading, that is, reading as a paradigm of God's nature and actions, may well lead in the direction of moral tales like Esther and Tobit. The second, the reading as ethical guidance, may lead towards materials such as the Testament literature. Both of these can be seen also in large elements of rabbinic Judaism. The third, the reading as a story with a direction, may be thought to lead towards the 'historical' rewriting of older scripture—to Chronicles and to Jubilees, for example; a more 'secular' approach of the same kind, more seriously historiographic in the Greek sense, can be seen in Josephus, who saw the entire body of prophets

(Former and Latter as we call them) as historians. The fourth, the predictive understanding, leads towards Qumran and towards Christianity.

Prediction in this type of understanding cut quite across the guidance of language and genre. It could apply to anything in scripture: even if a passage was referring to the past, it could be a prediction. By the canonical form of the passage, Hos. 11:1 'out of Egypt I called my son' is obviously a reference to the Exodus in the past, but Matt. 2:15 takes it unembarrassedly as a prediction, now fulfilled.[19] The prophets 'did not do this service for themselves but for you' (1 Pet. 1:12, my own translation), and the Christians are the ones 'upon whom the end of the ages has come' (1 Cor. 10:11).

All these four lines of reading were possible, and all were to some extent followed; they could be followed separately or in combination. Daniel, for instance, especially when seen in combination with the Greek Daniel tradition, embodies several of them. The same canon permitted them all, indeed the canon did nothing to adjudicate between one and another. The essential hermeneutic guide did not come from within the canon, but from without, from the priorities of the various directions that the religion might take and did take. And, just as the hermeneutic guidance is not given by the canonical form, so the evidence about the direction which interpretation took—the direction which enables canonical criticism, the study of how the books, taken as canon, were read, to proceed—is not provided from within the canon but from without. We cannot, by just looking at a text in the prophets and analysing it as modern scholars, or even as canonical critics, tell how that text would have been read and understood in 250 BC or 150 BC. Only evidence external to the text itself will tell us that. No one could have told from the book of Nahum, read for itself quite apart from all 'critical'

---

[19] This was often expounded as a good case of Exodus typology: Jesus was Israel coming forth from Egypt, he embodied in himself the meaning of the Exodus. I expect I have so argued myself. Though this may be in itself true on other grounds, it is not the point of the passage. Jesus' return from Egypt as a child is not compared to the Exodus. He is not in captivity there, but in safety, and his return is no deliverance comparable to the Exodus. For Matthew the passage is a prediction, the nucleus of which is the fact that it is 'my son' who is—in a quite un-Exodus-like journey—to come out of Egypt.

considerations, how the Qumran community would have read that book. Canonical criticism, in the sense of the perception of how the late community perceived and understood the balance and interrelations between the various elements in holy scripture as then existing, can be highly interesting and potentially fruitful; but it is heavily dependent on extracanonical evidence. In default of such evidence, we often have no choice but to remain silent.

We may add that something similar might be said of the New Testament canon. Contrary to the older idea that the New Testament, taken as a whole, provides a balance and acts as a criterion which might prove one of the forms of Christianity correct as against the others, it is now increasingly considered to contain the seeds of a number of different and potentially competing types of the faith. There are individual passages, strata, books or writers, which may clearly support one construction of Christianity as against another; but the canon as a whole does not. Rather, it contains the seeds of conflict.[20]

We may conclude this chapter by considering again the relation of historical and non-historical modes of reading the Bible. The last few paragraphs have indicated that the 'historical' books of the Old Testament were not necessarily read in a primarily historical mode. It has often been said that the emphasis on *historical* revelation comes primarily from the Old Testament and that the New Testament could easily be read unhistorically if it were not for the influence of the Old. Having doubtless said the same myself, I now think that it is mistaken. It is the Gospels that are the supreme source and the supreme problem area for historical revelation. It is in them that something is narrated of which one may say that, broadly speaking, if this did not happen, then there is no salvation and faith is vain. In Judaism the Torah, although absolutely central, does not necessarily work in that way.

---

[20] Cf. E. Käsemann's essay, 'Begründet der neutestamentliche Kanon die Einheit der Kirche?', in the volume edited by him, *Das Neue Testament als Kanon* (Göttingen: Vandenhoeck und Ruprecht, 1970), pp. 124–33. As a further example, one may say: the whole Protestant emphasis on the authority of scripture was rather vitiated by the failure to recognize the existence within scripture of elements which pointed in a Catholic direction.

Certainly in it we have (among others) a supreme and central event, the Exodus from Egypt, to which all Jews looked back as the pivot of their religion and to which each Jew sought to relate himself as if he had actually been there. But the centrality of this event did not alter the fact that the Torah as a whole worked in a different way: seen as a whole within Judaism, the Torah was read dominantly as a legal text. If it is of the nature of Christianity that it generates theology and doctrine, it is of the nature of Judaism that it generates law. Seen in this way, for Judaism as it has developed, the Torah is not primarily a report of or a witness to salvific events, which if they had not happened would have left man without salvation: rather, it is the divinely given *text*, essential for ritual worship and for the establishment of legal norms. In spite of the important narrative and historical material that it contains, the Torah could thus be seen and valued in a very non-historical way. Much of post-exilic Judaism was a very a-historical world, lacking in the sense of anachronism and reading back its (often recent) institutions into remote antiquity. The structure of Christianity was different. It was never a matter of having a perfect text. It is interesting and significant that Christianity, so far as we know, never sought to preserve the teaching of Jesus in the language in which he uttered it; from an early date it was a religion of which the most basic traditions existed only in translation.[21]

Christianity by contrast has depended much more on events, on the birth, death, and resurrection of Jesus; and the significance of his teaching lies primarily not in its use as a ritual text but in its conjunction with his life and work. Thus it should be perfectly understandable that the Old Testament could be read in a rather unhistorical way, even where it is to us very manifestly historical. Christianity, however, has within its own belief structure elements that must sooner or later pose serious historical problems. But the old Christian answers were never plain answers to historical questions,

---

[21] There are of course a few remarks which have been preserved in the Gospels in the original Hebrew or Aramaic but it cannot be said that these were particularly key sayings or that anything profoundly different is revealed by the preservation of the original language. Indeed, where the earlier Gospel, Mark, used the original language, the later ones like Matthew and Luke, following Mark, often dropped it.

because historical questions had never yet been isolated as specific questions. In spite of the presence in scripture of many narratives of historical type, certain aspects of historical enquiry had never become indigenous in the biblical or theological tradition: in particular, the question about the reliability of sources and reports, the question whether this or that report was true, even sometimes the full awareness of the difference between before and after. It was at the beginning of the modern period that historical questions came to be properly isolated and perceived. They were to some extent separated from their subordination to theological and metaphysical questions. It was thought possible to put the question: what does scripture itself say and what does it itself mean?—and in spite of qualification this is still a possible, a vital and an essential question today. The interpretation of scripture is a function of the language, the grammar and the literary genres. But the realization of this was not simply a derivative from the current reading techniques of early modern society. It derived also from an ultimate datum of Christian faith, the perception that its validity rested upon persons and events.

This point, in itself not so very original, is rehearsed here partly as a conclusion to what has been said about the various 'canonical' readings of the Prophets and partly also to sum up the discussion of this chapter and consider the *theological* values likely to be realized by new movements in interpretation. We began by considering how a biblical book might be read as it stands, without consideration of previous sources or of the circumstances of origin, perhaps even without consideration even of the intention of the author. Such a reading is certainly conceivable and indeed possible, and I would not be against it in principle. There remains the question whether such a type of interpretation could be *theologically* binding and authoritative. The evidence from modern movements of thought seems to point in the opposite direction. Although it may be perfectly possible to interpret the text in a way that disregards the historical perspectives and, taking the Bible as a corpus of self-contained material, interprets it purely along the lines of its own inner contours and its integral symbolism, it is doubtful whether this kind of interpretation is really very

significant for *theology*. On the contrary, it may often seem
more like a taking possession of the Bible by a perspective
that is ultimately non-theological. The support given by
modern literary studies to such a mode of reading may not be
a support from the viewpoint of *theology*; theology may be
endangered rather than enriched by such a support. Theology
as a mode of understanding comes into existence only when
one moves out of the plane of the text itself and begins to ask
about the extrinsic realities to which the text refers. It is very
peculiar therefore that it should be imagined that an
interpretation which remains immanent within the contours
of the text itself should be a *theologically* valuable exercise.

In spite of the many claims made by canonical criticism to
be a more truly *theological* approach to scripture than other
scholarly approaches have been, its actual product thus far
has shown no results that could be said to justify these claims.
Simply to *say* that it is more theological does not prove
anything. The only aspect of canonical criticism, as developed
up to the present time, that might justifiably claim to be really
theological seems to be its insistence that the starting point of
exegesis must be the Bible as it is, since it is to scripture as it is,
in its present form and defined by the canon, that Judaism
and the church offer allegiance. But no step in the actual
operation of canonical criticism can be described as genuinely
theological. It does not attempt to wrestle with the question of
truth. It does not tell us whether the view of God as presented
by, let us say, a prophetic book like Amos or Nahum, taken as
a whole, is true or adequate or not.[22] Or is it meant to imply
that we have no right to raise the question? Canonical
criticism, as it has worked out so far, appears to be not a
particularly theological operation but a sort of literary-
historical reading of a novel and unusual kind. It works, not

---

[22] Cf. McEvenue in *Interpretation* 35, 1981, 232ff. For another example, consider
Childs's argument about the 'pious fraud' theory of Deuteronomy in *JSOT* 16, 1980,
56. The 'pious fraud' theory, supposing the book to have been 'created for
propaganda reasons to support the political aspirations of the Jerusalem priesthood',
would create difficulties for a canonical interpretation 'which claimed that the book
was shaped by predominantly religious concerns'. 'For this reason' Childs feels
constrained to oppose this view. But what if the pious fraud theory is *true*? Should
not truth come first? If the pious fraud theory is true, then conceptions about the
canon will simply have to be modified. Actually it is difficult to see in what way

on the actual canonical form as it stands, but on the stages between the results of critical scholarship and the final form; in this sense, contrary to its theoretical assertions, it is historical, developmental, and genetic in type, sharing fully in the speculative weakness of traditional scholarship which it uses in its attacks upon the latter. Its actual perception of the canonical form appears to me to be very weak.[23] If the ideal of canonical criticism is to be *theology*, or to be *biblical theology*, it seems to fall more short of that ideal than the more traditional form of biblical theology, as exemplified by major writers like Eichrodt or von Rad.

It seems to me that, if a new direction in interpretation has to be taken up, there is much greater promise in something like structuralism or in the type of hermeneutic analysis offered by Ricoeur. Either of these has much greater philosophical coherence and power than canonical criticism as at present proposed. They may be criticized for being non-historical, but it is not clear that a historical element may not be built into them, and indeed, as has been pointed out above, it is possible that traditional historical criticism is explicable in structuralist terms.[24] In any case the criticism of these approaches for not being historical is one that cannot be used by canonical criticism, at least in Childs's version: the methods of the latter, as already indicated, are mainly historical and literary, and its difference from traditional criticism lies in its will to concentrate on a different *segment* of historical and literary development, namely the approach to the final text. But this shift of historical and literary interest to a different stage is accompanied by an extreme assault on the irrelevance, speculativeness, and theological uselessness of historical knowledge, and in this sense is a good example of the practice of cutting off the branch upon which one is

canonical criticism would be changed even if the theory was true: it would simply mean that the priests in question, knowing the importance of the canon, were using this way of making sure that this book became central in it. Much is revealed by the disclosure that the motivation is what matters: 'predominantly religious concerns'. But the history of the canon, as of scripture and theology generally, shows that religious concerns have very commonly been highly mixed with political ambitions throughout the centuries. The whole matter is highly revealing about attitudes to truth.
[23] Cf. above, pp. 90f., and below, p. 158.
[24] Cf. above, p. 86.

sitting.[25] Canonical criticism as it now stands, far from being the genuinely theological approach, lies in an uneasy balance between the historical, the literary, and the theological, unable to accept any one of them completely and unwilling to cut loose completely from any of them either.

The more general theological issues, however, will be followed up in the next chapter. It is possible, as some have thought, that the design of canonical criticism aims not at theological interpretation of scripture but at one particular theology, a theology the central and dominant feature of which is the stance taken towards scripture.[26] I wonder whether the real appeal of canonical criticism is not an appeal to religion, to religious sentiments and instincts, rather than an interest in evaluative theology. Because it takes the Bible as it stands and the books as they stand, and because it leaves aside as irrelevant the historical, sociological, and other approaches, it feels like a truly religious and devoted way of handling scripture. In spite of its highly academic and critical intellectual apparatus, therefore, it is possible that it might have a popular appeal to the religious such as previous forms of critical scholarship have not had. Religiosity, however, is not the same thing as theology. Theology begins when we pass by the sense of religious satisfaction and begin to pose the question of truth.

[25] Cf. above, p. 78n. It seems to me that Childs, in criticizing Ricoeur's ideas because they show 'no interest in the historical development of the biblical text or even in the historical context of the canonical text', is undercutting his own entire position. Why, on Childs's terms, *should* Ricoeur be interested in these historical developments and contexts? If he has read Childs, he will have learned that historical context is theologically irrelevant. If historical development is right for Ricoeur, why should it be wrong for those who want to know what were the ideas of the prophet Amos? In any case I think Childs reads Ricoeur's thinking wrongly: Ricoeur is far more interested in historical study, and far more positive towards its values, than Childs is. Cf. again below, p. 159.

[26] See Appendix II, in which I discuss in more detail the present situation of canonical criticism and its bibliography.

V

The spiritual and intellectual basis of modern biblical research

THE wide-ranging issues that have been discussed lead us to consider afresh the general picture of biblical scholarship in its relation to the entire intellectual scene, especially as it has changed through the Renaissance, the Reformation, and the Enlightenment. And I have chosen my terms, 'modern biblical research', carefully. In particular I have avoided the term 'historical criticism', for 'historical criticism', contrary to much present opinion, is much too narrow and limited a term to indicate how scholars handle and interpret the Bible. As was already argued above,[1] biblical criticism is not one method, nor even a group of methods. Nor is it necessarily primarily historical in character. The basis of biblical criticism seems to me to be essentially literary and linguistic, rather than historical, in character. Its basic perceptions seem to derive from the Renaissance, with its renewed ability to read ancient texts as literature, to perceive literary genres and relate them to the details of language and thereby to find the path to interpretation. It is therefore more true to say that biblical criticism is a literary mode of operation, which carries with it historical consequences, than to say that it is a historical mode of operation, which carries with it literary consequences. It is therefore not at all correct to suppose that biblical criticism represents the acceptance of the secular discipline of history and the enthronement of history as the controlling factor in the understanding of the Bible. Many of the traditional critical disciplines are only in a limited sense historical in their character: form-criticism, for instance, as the term has generally been understood, is hardly historical at all. The decisions by which one may judge that 2 Peter was not written by Simon Peter or Ephesians not written by St. Paul are scarcely historical judgements. The judgement that

[1] See above, pp. 33f.

the Elihu speeches form some sort of foreign body within the text of Job is a linguistic and literary judgement, not a historical one. The rise of biblical criticism, far from being an imitation and consequence of the rise of modern historical science, in many ways preceded the latter, so that biblical criticism was as creative in the development of historical research as history was in inspiring biblical study. The idea that biblical criticism is a child of historicism is very wide of the mark. Biblical criticism depends more completely on relations between part and whole, between small-scale linguistic form and large-scale literary form. All this is important, because we increasingly hear voices today that tell us that theology in the last century or so has laid too much weight upon history and that the paradigm for biblical studies in the future will be something more like literature than like history. This may or may not be right. But, if it should be true, it will not mean that the place of biblical criticism will thereby be undermined: on the contrary, literary and linguistic criteria, properly applied, may well reinforce the soundness of the tradition of biblical criticism.

There were good reasons, however, why the *historical* aspects and consequences of biblical criticism quickly came into the foreground. The first lay in the nature of Christianity as to an unusual degree a historical religion.[2] It depended on essential saving events located in the past, and something of these events was narrated in the Bible. Critical studies of the language and literary character of the texts had effects upon their character and quality as historical narration, and therefore had effects upon our idea of the knowledge we might have of the events themselves. In this respect the importance of *historical* criticism derived not from the prestige of history but from the historical character of the Christian religion itself. Secondly, among the various products of criticism its historical results, or some of them, were particularly clear in formulability and thus particularly visible as indicators. Certain key discoveries, such as the

---

[2] This assertion about the nature of Christianity is, I admit, capable of several different meanings, but it is not necessary to disentangle them here; I attempt to do so in my *Explorations in Theology 7*, pp. 31–5.

separateness of Deutero-Isaiah or the late date of Daniel, decisively altered our picture of what the Bible was like. The sort of thing that is now regarded as an advanced hermeneutic insight, for instance that the Gospels do not present the very words of Jesus but the early church's authoritative interpretation of him, would never have been thought of but for the historical effects of critical study. The manifold uncertainties of historical reconstruction within the biblical period do not alter the magnitude of the difference that it has made. The difference is made, not by the achievement of certainty, but by the perception of probability, and even by the envisaging of likelihood. The historical aspects of criticism, therefore, achieved a great deal of notice, and in Protestantism it followed naturally upon the fact, mentioned above, that a certain historical criticism of the Roman Catholic picture of the tradition was already well established in the learning of the Reformation.[3] The prominence of the historical aspects, however, should not be taken to show that historical science was the ideal upon which biblical criticism modelled itself. Certainly many of the defenders of biblical criticism tried to justify it, especially later, on the ground that it was historical; and this in turn laid the subject open to the charge that, as 'the historical-critical method', it was no more than a mere method, and that one derived by mere imitation from historical science.[4]

I also used the term 'biblical research' intentionally. Here again we are dealing not with a method or with a particular line of investigation, but with the entire universe of discourse in which scholarly knowledge of the Bible is advanced and maintained. Not all such research is truly 'critical', for

---

[3] Cf. above, p. 36.

[4] Thus one hears voices which speak with secret pleasure of the 'end of the historical-critical method', and this could of course be argued quite well, though one could not say it is well argued by Gerhard Maier, *The End of the Historical-critical Method* (St. Louis: Concordia, 1977), a work so ignorant in its assertions and so weak in its reasoning that its very existence constitutes a support to the method the end of which it celebrates. It is doubtful whether it deserves the careful reply of P. Stuhlmacher, *Historical Criticism and Theological Interpretation of Scripture* (London: SPCK, 1979), pp. 66–71. The wild, thoughtless, and journalistic work of W. Wink, *The Bible in Human Transformation* (Philadelphia: Fortress, 1973) is not much different. In fact all serious criticism of historical criticism in modern times has come from people like Ebeling and Stuhlmacher who basically fully affirm its great positive importance.

criticism implies freedom,[5] and there is much scholarship which feels itself bound to reach the results required by this or that religious tradition and which in this sense is not critical. The universe of biblical research seems to me, however, clearly to comprehend both types. Many methods and perspectives are held in common, and the scholarly community, with its societies and institutions, is also one. The leading edge in research and new knowledge is commonly critical, but very important new insights can also equally well be discovered by non-critical study. It is important to observe the extent of this common ground, because many features of modern biblical research which are attributed, with blame or with praise, to critical study actually belong to the entire climate of biblical scholarship. It is critical study, however, that poses the most interesting issues to be discussed in what follows.

There is a further aspect intended by the use of the word 'research'. For critical scholarship the standard and criterion for judging the validity of exegesis lies no longer in church doctrine, but in research. It might seem that this would provoke a conflict with church authority, but in fact this has happened relatively seldom. On the whole biblical criticism and traditional doctrine have succeeded in living remarkably well together. It was mainly late in the development of criticism, and rather seldom, that heresy trials and the like were resorted to, chiefly at the end of the nineteenth century: Robertson Smith, Briggs, Loisy. Far from it being the case that biblical criticism introduced and encouraged an orgy of anticonfessional libertinism, critical scholars have been much more worthy of blame for being excessively governed and guided by the ruling trends of their own confessional tradition. Bultmann is an obvious example: for surely his entire theological position can be plausibly read as deriving from a profound and extreme application of the Lutheran understanding of justification by faith. If he thought that faith should not be built upon the reliability of historical reports about the life of Christ, this was not (as Anglo-Saxon critics have often supposed) a result of 'historical scepticism', but

[5] For further thoughts along this line see my article 'Bibelkritik als theologische Aufklärung' in T. Rendtorff (ed.), *Glaube und Toleranz. Das theologische Erbe der Aufklärung* (Munich, 1982).

because faith itself would be in danger of destruction if it relied upon such a support. The well-known association over a certain time between biblical criticism and liberal theology is also to be understood thus: powerful currents in the church became liberal, biblical critics became liberal too. When, later, neo-orthodoxy began to overcome the liberal tradition, biblical scholars (often after some delay) started to make a similar change in direction: the rise of 'biblical theology' was the obvious example. There was another reason why the clash with confessional doctrine was often avoided: the questions raised by biblical criticism were commonly questions to which traditional church doctrine had no answer, indeed it had not known that the questions existed. To such questions as the date of Deuteronomy, the cultic interpretation of the Psalms or the relations between Mark and Luke, bishops, popes, moderators, creeds, and confessions had no official answer, commonly no answer at all. Basically it was accepted that the answers were to be found by research: only marginally was it possible to pre-empt the decision of research by the authority of church or confession. More important, however, the place of research at the heart of scholarship meant that the context of biblical understanding was no longer alone the church as such: the context had also to be the total academic community, and this is true whether study is carried out in church-related institutions or in universities which have no special church relationship or indeed are completely secular. Whether related to a church or not, the academic institution was not in itself a church. It was the Enlightenment in particular that perceived and ensured this. And, with the increasingly manifold character of knowledge, both in humanities and in sciences, this made it clear that theology itself could no longer count as the sole and absolute criterion for the evaluation of biblical studies; biblical studies must draw upon other disciplines and be carried out in relation to them.

The thought of research brings us back again to the importance of freedom.[6] Research requires freedom of

---

[6] In those matters I acknowledge stimulus from the Wilde Lectures delivered in Oxford by Professor J.D.M. Derrett.

thought; if this is lacking, it only means that the research will be less good, in extreme cases that it will dry up altogether. Freedom is not something that should have to be wrung from a reluctant grasp: the church should promote freedom, because freedom is part of its gospel. The same is true of theology: it is in the interests of theology itself that it should not seek the power to control and limit, that it should recognize, accept, and promote the fact that there are regions of biblical study for which the criteria of theology are not appropriate; just as it is salutary for the church that it should not seek to dominate the nature of education. When these freedoms are not freely given, then secular concepts of freedom through human rights become better. The relations between freedom and religion are paradoxical. Freedom *of* religion is one thing, freedom *within* religion is another. Freedom of religion is often thought of as freedom of religion from coercion through the state, and that can sometimes be very important, though it is far from being the nucleus of the idea of Christian freedom. Religions can demand freedom *of* religion, while denying freedom *within* religion, which is much closer to the idea of Christian freedom. However, we cannot pursue these thoughts here. Though seldom recognized or properly considered, they are part of the setting and basis of modern biblical research.

This brings us to the often-discussed question of motivation and commitment. The Christian biblical scholar has as his God-given task the study of scripture. He does it not as a mere secular job but in the consciousness that he is handling the Word of God and that what he is doing is of immense practical and spiritual importance for the church. This is his motivation and his commitment. But he recognizes that perfectly valid and constructive biblical study, positively significant for theology and church, can be carried out and is carried out by scholars who do not share this motivation, and he welcomes this as a gift of God in the interpretation of scripture, even when the scholars concerned may be quite lacking in religious interest. The recognition of such valid non-theologically-motivated biblical scholarship is not a grudging negative aspect: rather, it is a positive recognition of the freedom of the scripture to address us other than through the mediation of our own tradition. For the Christian scholar his study, and especially his critical study, belongs to his Christian commitment, but he recognizes and welcomes the fact and the validity of study done without such commitment. It follows that the presence or absence of personal religious commitment cannot function as a test of the validity of methods or results.

This point fits in well with our theme, for one of the claims advanced by recent canonical criticism is that biblical theology, and by implication also analysis of the literature, must begin from a position of religious commitment, which would perceive the material as canonical scripture, authoritative in the community. If this was seriously meant it would follow that biblical scholarship would be divided into two sharply distinct groups, one working from within religious commitment and the other not. It is in fact very unlikely that canonical critics want this; but if they do not want it then their insistence on religious commitment as a basis for biblical study is simply futile. Actually, in any case, canonical criticism as it has been thus far developed has no essential connection with commitment at all. Anyone, whether religious or not, can do canonical criticism: the only commitment requisite is an interest in doing this sort of critical work. To perceive that the Bible is canonical Christian scripture, or canonical Jewish scripture, is an insight attainable by anyone, with or without any personal involvement in the Jewish or Christian religions. No aspect that is really dependent on personal religious commitment is built into the structure or proceedings of canonical criticism. In this respect its position is not different from that of traditional biblical criticism. It may well be, of course, that persons of religious commitment will look with more favour upon canonical criticism; but the idea that the actual practice of it is dependent upon religious commitment is an illusion.

To the opponents of biblical criticism, nothing is more irritating than the notion that it is neutral, objective, free from presuppositions, and in this sense scientific. Biblical criticism is pictured by many of its opponents, in other words, according to the popular theological image of positivism. On the contrary, people think, there must be presuppositions, which is doubtless true. But as an argument against biblical criticism this reasoning has little power. As has already been indicated, biblical criticism was seldom fuelled by the positivist gospel, much more was it motivated by the contemporary problems of theology and by the overriding drive to understand the Bible. Those who hope to cast doubt upon biblical criticism by deploying the Dilthey-Gadamer series of arguments about the differences between the humanities and the physical sciences are therefore deeply mistaken: biblical criticism never belonged other than to the humanities in its methods and inspiration. Only late in the development of biblical criticism, and probably only in the United States with its high evaluation of scientific objectivity, was the model of the sciences much used as the image of biblical scholarship. The motivation behind biblical scholarship derived overwhelmingly from theology and from the conviction of the authority of scripture. Few or no critics really treated the Bible as if it was, in the customary phrase, just 'any other book'; their whole procedure demonstrated the presupposition that there was something uniquely important about this particular book.

The question of presuppositions, however, is not as important as it sounds, and is highly paradoxical and contradictory. Presuppositions are one thing, how one handles the evidence is another. One may have right presuppositions and come to the wrong conclusions; one may have quite mistaken presuppositions and come to the right conclusions. In any case traditional theology was in no position to tell biblical scholarship what the right presuppositions were: for on many questions it had no presuppositions, right or wrong, to offer, as already remarked, while on others the presuppositions it had to offer were contrary to the actual data of the biblical text. What is generally meant, when people speak about presuppositions, is that they want deductive considerations, based upon a few texts like 2 Tim. 3:16 plus purely deductive reasonings with these texts as departure point, to be imposed as authoritative upon the inductive study of the vast mass of the material. It was critical scholarship, and not its opponents, that worked from the material of scripture as a whole; but its mode of work was such as to create new alignments—sources, glosses, parallels —which had not been evident on the surface form of the text.

The real operating force in biblical research, far from a scientific neutrality and objectivity, has been something more like what we could call 'creative prejudice'. Far from disregarding theological forces, critical scholars were if anything too much guided by them. But—and here is another limitation of the stress upon presuppositions—the results of critical scholarship turned out not to be tied to the motivations and influences which had guided it. Thus the forces and influences of liberal theology gave many important suggestions to criticism; but many of these results were seen to remain after liberal theology had largely departed, and were acceptable to many who repudiated the entire ideological apparatus of liberalism. The same is true, conversely, of fundamentalism: the peculiar drives and interests of fundamentalist scholarship have at times led it to discern and identify things that no one else would have noticed or evaluated properly. And the same can be said of a new movement like canonical criticism: there is no reason to doubt that its peculiar prejudices will lead it to uncover things that but for it would never have been noticed.

But in another respect biblical criticism *has had* a considerable degree of scientific objectivity. Unlike most theology, it has not been sectarian. As I have said, far from asserting freedom from their confessional traditions, many biblical critics were too much influenced by them; but at least their work took place within an interdenominational context and it did not take denominational allegiance as a criterion or as a test of validity. When theology was regarded, in many universities, as non-scientific, this was not so much because it was not a natural science—after all philosophy, an equally ideological subject, seldom suffered from this objection—but because it was sectarian. Churches insisted that theology must be Anglican theology, Baptist theology, Catholic theology. The university as such could not be expected to judge on what was authentic Baptist theology or authentic Methodist theology: it had no criteria for doing so. In this sense theology seemed to people to be non-scientific. Critical study of the Bible, on the other hand, was comparatively free from this weakness and counted therefore as more 'scientific'. As has been already remarked, it was precisely this characteristic of biblical criticism that showed that it was not mere Protestant propaganda and enabled its eventual acceptance within the Roman Catholic community to take place.[7] Critical biblical scholarship *is* objective in the sense that its results are not predetermined by a given authoritative ideology.

Another of the aspects of biblical criticism is the widespread feeling that it is overwhelmingly analytic in method and interest. It divided books up into sources, and discovered glosses, later insertions, redactional additions, and the like everywhere. This is of course true, and works like 'introductions', which concentrated on literary analysis, displayed how much this was so. It is certainly true that most traditional critical work, as canonical critics have pointed out, showed a certain lack of interest in the final form of the books as they stand. But in another way biblical criticism was always synthetic: it strove towards a comprehensive account of the material; if it divided, it also put back together. Indeed, if one were to offer a hostile review of biblical criticism, one might well say that its way of putting together was more questionable than its analytical procedures. Moreover, the work of biblical criticism is not fairly assessed unless we also include the work of biblical theology, the theology of the Old and New Testaments, the theology of individual biblical writers like Luke, that was done on a critical basis. All this work was unquestionably synthetic in character, and some of it produced a very impressive synthetic picture.[8] It is at the moment highly unlikely that canonical criticism can produce a theological picture of equal depth and power.

It is certainly true, as canonical criticism has claimed, that traditional biblical criticism stood somewhat in the shadow of the dominating concept of the 'original', that it looked more to the beginnings than to the results and effects, and that the

---

[7] Cf. above, pp. 30f.

[8] Thus, if we are to compare the advantages promised by canonical criticism with the situation present before its rise, one would have to compare it not with the *Einleitungswissenschaft* alone but with the combination of the latter with Old Testament and New Testament theology, plus history of religion and other aspects; see my remarks in *JSOT* 16, 1980, 20.

Nachgeschichte and *Wirkungsgeschichte* of the biblical texts was somewhat neglected, indeed seriously neglected. More account of this ought to be taken, and I have long thought and said so myself. Nevertheless there may also be some good reasons why critical scholarship tended to build up its picture of the materials by starting from the original; one has already been suggested above.[9] But, agreeing that greater emphasis on the after-history of the biblical text is needed, the effect of this, paradoxically, is to drive us all the more back to a rigorously historical-critical approach: for, even if other approaches to the books themselves are possible, the knowledge of their after-history is unquestionably a historical-critical matter. There is nothing in the methods or interests of traditional historical criticism that makes it unable to perform this task: on the contrary, it is the sort of task it is uniquely well equipped to perform. If it does not perform it, it may well be because the data are lacking. We cannot tell what was the after-history of texts by simple guesswork or divination from the texts themselves, or by deduction from our ideas about the canon. In fact, where canonical criticism has made good and valid statements about the after-history of texts, they have never differed in quality from traditional historical criticism and have been good and valid on exactly this ground. The difference, if any, has lain only in the motivation for the focusing of interest in this direction.

It is often thought that biblical criticism conduces to a contempt of pre-critical interpretation, and no doubt this has often been so. Actually, pre-critical interpretation is often intensely interesting and rewarding. More important still, much of the doctrinal structure of traditional Christianity depends upon pre-critical exegesis, one must even say on wrong exegesis, wrong not in the sense of different from critical exegesis, but wrong by the criteria which even older theology applied. This is no new situation. Reformational theology deplored allegorization, but it maintained forms of ancient orthodoxy which had been constructed only through the use of allegory. The rejection of allegory was made more difficult also by the presence of allegorization, even if only

[9] Cf. above, pp. 84–91.

limited in extent, within the New Testament itself. Our Lord's remarks in interpretation of Old Testament passages have authority for us because he spoke them, but it is often difficult for us to say that they can count as right interpretations of the text or, in other words, it is difficult or impossible for us to universalize them and draw from them a principle or method which we could affirm as our own. I have already studied these questions,[10] and would still say what I then said: that methods such as typology and allegory partake to some extent in the once-ness of the incarnation: the structure of Christianity was built up not merely by the Bible but also by a certain period in the process of its interpretation. Respect for traditional interpretation is therefore enjoined upon us. Yet it is doubtful whether there is any current in modern scholarship which feels able to make the principles and procedures of pre-critical exegesis its own. Certainly modern canonical criticism does not: its methods stand entirely upon the ground established by older critical scholarship, and its attacks on the character and achievements of that older scholarship thus constitute a kind of suicidal self-destruction. Its entirely justified sympathetic interest in pre-critical scholarship makes no real difference to its working methods.

The real core of canonical criticism, at least in Childs's form of it, seems to be its conception of exegesis as a *purely* theological undertaking. Theological exegesis is related directly to the canonical text and to it only. We may by various methods discern factors extrinsic to the text, such as previous sources, historical circumstances, character of likely audiences, intentions of the authors, stage of religious development at which events occurred, and so on; but these, though they may be true, are regarded as not strictly relevant to theological interpretation and indeed divert the attention from it. All these other kinds of information are at best ancillary: even after they are known and recognized, theological interpretation starts again at the bottom, with only the canonical text itself.[11] Theology does not take up into itself the

[10] Cf. *Old and New in Interpretation* (London: SCM, 1966), pp. 131ff.
[11] This position seems akin to the argument of Kelsey, op. cit., p. 199: 'By definition, exegesis₁ and exegesis₂ [i.e. study that seeks historical reconstruction and study that seeks to elucidate the author's intentions and the way in which the original audience

results of independent disciplines, it is a distinct operation working by theological criteria only. In fact, however, as has been already indicated, the theological nature of canonical criticism is aspiration rather than actuality.[12] Moreover, I think that the understanding of theology as a purely theological discipline is itself a thoroughly mistaken one: incidentally, it is also an understanding quite discontinuous with the tradition of pre-critical exegesis, which took up into itself a vast input from other disciplines, especially from philosophy. Theology is never pure theology. It lives and depends upon a multitude of forms of information which belong to, and can be understood only through, disciplines which are not theological in their nature. Even the assertions of systematic and doctrinal theologians are seldom purely theological in their nature, for they depend on, and are expressed by means of, opinions on the level of the history of ideas; and matters in the history of ideas, though commonly very important for theology, can neither be proved by, nor are dependent on, theological positions themselves.[13] Theology may be pictured as the apex of a pyramid, the lower levels of which consist of non-theological, or semi-theological, bodies of fact, and are controlled by non-theological, or semi-theological, disciplines; and what is decided at the ultimate theological level is in many respects dependent upon what is judged to be possible at these lower, not fully theological, levels. An obvious example is the case of language;[14] the meaning of a linguistic item is its meaning in contrast to the meanings of other terms which might have existed in the same language at the same time. But these other meanings commonly lie outside the biblical canon: yet the meanings of the biblical words are known only where these other meanings are taken into consideration. Biblical language is a language shared by the canonical writings with a milieu that lies beyond the canon, not only the milieu of the 'apocryphal'

would have understood it] cannot of themselves help scripture function normatively in doing theology, for they are study of biblical texts as texts and precisely not as "scripture".' But, if this is so 'by definition', surely it only shows that the definition was wrong in the first place.

[12] Cf. above, p. 102.
[13] Cf. *Explorations in Theology 7*, p. 27.
[14] Cf. already above, pp. 85ff.

writings, which in this respect differ only a little, but the milieu of the false prophets, the milieu of the opponents of St. Paul. Grammar is not under the control of the canon; nor is it under the control of theology. Theology is indebted to it; but it cannot, as theology, do anything to govern it. The position of language is perhaps the clearest—Luther himself noted with interest the critical role exercised by 'grammar', as he called it, in exegesis; but it is only the leading one in a variety of disciplines which similarly bear upon the understanding of scripture.[15] Theological exegesis is at all points built upon non-theological or semi-theological material; and it always was so.

To this must be added another point: the final criterion for theology cannot be relevance: it can only be truth. Recent hermeneutical discussions have emphasized the concept of relevance, and it is indeed not without importance. But relevance cannot compete with the overriding primacy of truth. If it is *true* that Isaiah 40–66 was composed in the exilic period, it is immensely important and therefore relevant and—taken along with other facts of the same kind—it effects a massive change in our picture of what sort of work the Bible is. It may of course not be true: and one must fully respect as a serious argument any argument that it is not true. But if it is true it cannot be otherwise than enormously relevant. Childs affirms 'the legitimacy of the historical critical enterprise'. Of course he does. But legitimacy is not much. Legitimacy may indeed be practically nothing: for it may conceal a decision by which that which is legitimate, and even true, is excluded from any role of importance. What matters is not legitimacy, but the ability of theology to recognize, and in some cases to recognize as decisive, truth that has become known through a process not purely theological, and to make room within its own understanding for that recognition. Thus, for instance, the perception of a sociological situation that lies behind a biblical text and in effect generates it is not at all inappropriate or improper as an approach to the text, nor is it irrelevant to theology. Such a perception may indeed be speculative or

---

[15] It is thus no accident that canonical criticism has been developed by scholars with a background in form criticism or hermeneutics rather than language; cf. below, pp. 139f., 142–6.

mistaken—I suspect that most of them are—but if it is *true* then it is entirely proper and relevant for theological exegesis. *For theology everything that is true is relevant.* Some truths are more remote than others: but those that are more remote have their effect upon those that are closer. Ugaritic language is not as close as Hebrew language; but what happens in Ugaritic studies must have an effect on what is known in Hebrew studies. There is no limit in principle to the network of relevance for theology.

This leads us on to the question of biblical theology itself. Unlike many scholars, and in spite of many criticisms I have made of many arguments that have been used within biblical theology, I continue to think that there is such a discipline and that it can render a useful service. It cannot, however, by its nature be 'theological' in the full sense of the word. Its service is rather ancillary and preparatory. It is not at the summit of the pyramid but a little way down. It is not in a position to make the ultimate decisions. From the empirical materials, such as language and textual studies, and from the various kinds of exegesis, it assembles the structures that seem—in a preparatory manner—to be most likely to be of more direct theological importance. But its work is character- ized by two major features. One is non-finality. The ultimate decisions of theology cannot be taken by biblical theology alone, but can be taken only when all the relevant factors have been considered: and these factors include systematic questions, moral considerations and philosophical perspec- tives which lie beyond the scope of any biblical theology. A proper theological education—such as is finely exemplified by a great and noble institution such as Union Theological Seminary in Richmond—brings together these various factors through the contributions of different professors and depart- ments. Only through the consideration of all of these is the point of true theological decision reached. In respect of the ideas of the canon this means: even if it were true—as I suggest it is not—that the canon was the determining guideline for biblical theology, this would still not mean that the canon was the determining guideline for theology as such. Biblical theology cannot wisely decide its own questions without considering what theology as a whole will require, nor can it salutarily insist that its own priorities must override all other considerations.

Moreover, because biblical theology does not stand at the culminating summit of theology, and therefore cannot make ultimate decisions, biblical theology must accept the possibility, and the fact, of variation within itself. There can be, and there must be, a variety of seriously possible biblical theologies. Since biblical theology is partial, and does not view the entire field of divinity, and since it cannot make final decisions on a theological level, it has to accept that it contains within itself no means of making absolute decisions between one proposal and another. Different views, not only of the final outlines of a biblical theology, but also of the very principles upon which the subject may be approached, have always existed and will always exist. In respect of the ideas of canonical criticism this means: if this aspires, as it has done, to be a valid method within biblical theology, its only likely chance of success is if it accepts the validity of other approaches also, and the validity of their results. No one will seriously suppose that canonical criticism will produce, let us say, theologies of the Old Testament that will be the equal of the works constructed by Eichrodt or by von Rad; it has not even taken the first step in that direction. If there is a chance for something good and permanent to come out of canonical criticism, it will be only if it begins to acknowledge that the work done under these other methods has equal validity with (or higher validity than) that done under its own, and if it thus begins to see itself as integrating the results of other approaches rather than replacing them with its own.[16]

These remarks about biblical research and its relation to theology cannot be concluded, however, without some reference to another matter; namely, the fact that theology, as

[16] See already above, p. 114. This matter is the worst aspect of the misrepresentation by Childs of the modern scholarly tradition to which he himself belongs. In the hands of men like von Rad the analytic approach of scholarship was fully accepted; but it ran out into a massive synthetic structure, such as canonical criticism is not likely to parallel. This was no exceptional case: it was in many ways the dominant pattern over a considerable time. A case like that of von Rad shows that all the assaults on critical scholarship for objectivism, descriptivism, lack of theological perspective and failure to bring things together for the needs of the church's proclamation were untrue. On this see again below, pp. 170ff.

theology, must be critical. Criticism is not to be narrowly thought of as an attribute of a particular element in biblical study: rather, criticism belongs to theology as a whole. By criticism, when used of theology, I mean this: that the establishment of theological truth does not take place by a mere passive acceptance of data given by the sources of revelation, but takes place through a critical and estimative weighing of these data. The theologian asks 'Is this true?' and in doing so he asks '*Why* is this true?' Naturally, he is under the authority of the sources that are authoritative for his thinking; but he is not under their authority in such a way that he has no right to question or to criticize. Questioning and criticism is his task, given by God and performed on behalf of the church. Theology itself therefore must be critical; and, seen from the side of theology, its own critical nature is a much more important matter than the so-called 'historical criticism' of the biblical books.

Modern critical theology, however, arose at about the same time and under the same circumstances as modern biblical criticism arose. It is a curious fault that so much attention has been directed at biblical criticism, when the major change, as one passes into the modern period, came not from biblical criticism but from critical theology. Most of the great changes that occurred did not derive from analysis of books, dating of sources and the like: rather, they came from a change in the conditions under which people were prepared to believe. In the seventeenth century, for instance, Methuselah was still simply a man, who had lived 969 years. Because the Bible stated this, it was a historical fact. The Bible stated no reasons why it should be important or what conclusions one should drawn from it; but it was clearly a historical fact, and God would not have told us it unless it had some importance. 'Historical criticism' in the traditional sense did nothing that affected Methuselah's long life: there was no question of differing sources, and, whatever the date of the author, whether it was Moses or someone else, he had still said 969 years. What made the difference in the eighteenth century was not biblical criticism as such, but a more critical theological attitude to the sources of all belief, of which the Bible was first or at least central. Various new kinds of information—which came from quite outside the biblical books themselves and the exegesis of them—made people no longer ready passively to believe that Methuselah simply lived 969 years. If they were told that the Christian faith required them to believe this, they now simply laughed: it was obviously ludicrous. To believe that Christ had died and risen for the forgiveness of sins, yes; to believe that Methuselah lived 969 years, no—it could no longer be believed that the latter stood on the same level. The affirmations of scripture stood no longer on the same level: they had to be weighed and estimated critically. There was therefore no longer one equal level for all biblical materials. And, this being so, the question of the intentionality of the Methuselah tradition could begin to be asked: what did the writer or writers *intend*, what theological truth were they seeking to convey, when they wrote about this man? Only when it became evident that Methuselah might be legend, rather than historical fact, could the question of intentionality be asked. The change of attitude came not from historical criticism, but from a newer theological orientation, which had become critical towards its materials. When people in modern times blame 'historical criticism' for separating the university from the church, the preacher from the Bible, and the Bible from its relevance for today, they are usually not thinking of biblical criticism at all: the cause of the troubles they bewail is the different attitude of people to ultimate theological questions. Against this fact any reorientation on the purely biblical level—whether rejection of biblical criticism, or new designs for biblical theology, or attempts at new constellations of the types of criticism—is of no real importance.

In summing up this series of lectures I want to recall something of the historical setting. I think in particular of two sets of events which took place roughly two hundred years ago. These events are relevant to our theme because they are events of the time we call the Enlightenment. Why, we may ask, should this matter? It matters because traditional biblical criticism, as we have known it, though in many ways (as I have maintained) a child of the Reformation, is a child that was brought to birth at the Enlightenment. And, unless I am mistaken, the movement of canonical criticism, as we have seen it in recent times, can be understood as very much an attempt to dispose of the Enlightenment, to destroy its values and drive out its way of dealing with biblical materials. According to this view, the Reformation was a good time, and pre-critical exegesis in general has great values to offer, but the Enlightenment introduced a damaging and distorting set of questions. One could not say that this, if meaningful at all, was because it introduced the idea of history—actually the Enlightenment was not so very historical in its orientation—but rather it made more familiar the idea of religion, as distinct from theology, and with it the notion of pluralism in religion. There was only one God, but there were different human ideas of God, different religions. If a man claimed 'My God is the true God', this was now seen as nothing different from saying 'This picture of God is my religion'. There were thus different pictures of God among men. This fact could then be transferred to the Bible: different strata within the Bible could now be seen as expressions of different sets of religious ideas. This possibility was an essential element in the approach of biblical criticism. It introduced a comparative element, which was in many ways earlier and more fundamental than the historical emphasis, which has so often been regarded as the chief characteristic of biblical criticism. Religion differed: it had changed and developed, and so the difference between religious ideas, within the Bible as outside it, could be understood as a sequence.

Was the Enlightenment wrong in all this? The first of the two events I want to mention was the Edict of Religious Toleration of the Emperor Joseph II of Austria in 1781. It reminds us of something that was once very profoundly important for the Protestant consciousness: the position of Protestants in a dominantly Catholic country, the life of a Protestant minority in the midst of a great Catholic majority. In such situations Protestantism was always highly conscious of the values of freedom, of the claim for religious toleration. Where Protestantism was in the majority, or thought itself to be so, the values of toleration and the positive claims of freedom have often been less clearly perceived. Early in the Reformation period, Austria came close to becoming a Protestant country: the Catholic church was in a state of disorganization, its institutions were almost empty and without direction, Lutheranism and Calvinism along with other Protestant options seemed to be on the increase.[17] But the counter-reformation was highly successful in Austria, and revived Roman Catholicism soon gained an overwhelming social and political ascendancy. It was the Emperor who was inspired by ideas of the Enlightenment, Joseph II, who relieved Protestants (and also Jews) of much of the burden of their inferior status. The current of ideas from which all this sprang included also the beginnings of biblical criticism. At a congress which celebrated the bicentenary of the Edict of Toleration, in 1981, I was invited to deliver one of the chief lectures, and the theme suggested was 'biblical criticism as theological enlightenment'. The rethinking of historical experience that went into that work forms part of the basis of the present book.[18] Biblical criticism was one part of that total shift in the history of ideas, out of which the acceptance of religious toleration came.

The other event in my mind, from more or less the same epoch, is the American Declaration of Independence. Much American religion, both Catholic and Protestant, has been, one feels, unhappy about the Enlightenment and the effects it had on Bible and religion. Surely, one might say, the Enlightenment was only one historical phenomenon, that lasted for a time but is explicable in terms of the social context of that time and cannot be expected to last for ever? Cannot one therefore cut loose from it and return to some earlier and purer time like the seventeenth century? Surely no historical circumstance lasts for ever? But it is difficult for Americans in particular to be so critical of the Enlightenment. For the greatest single social document of the Enlightenment—in its effects and its ramifications far exceeding the Austrian Edict of Toleration—is without doubt the Constitution of the United States. And the Constitution is not just a historical

---

[17] On this see R.J.W. Evans, *The Making of the Habsburg Monarchy, 1550–1700* (Oxford University Press, 1979). The first sentence of the book, p. 3, is: 'By the middle of the sixteenth century the ethos of the Austrian Habsburg lands was Protestant.'

[18] The paper will be published as 'Bibelkritik als theologische Aufklärung' in T. Rendtorff, *Glaube und Toleranz. Das theologische Erbe der Aufklärung.*

document of the past: it was made to last, and it has lasted. Although it can be amended, it has been amended very little. No major country of the world has had so little constitutional change over the last two hundred years as the United States. And, quite apart from constitutional legality, people like it that way: as a foreigner, I hear comparatively few Americans complaining about the Constitution, or saying that it is a bad one and ought to be scrapped from top to bottom and replaced with something different. And surely this is part of the reason for certain religious tensions: that the state and the social milieu derive many of their values from the Enlightenment, at the same time as much of the religion feels doubtful of these values or opposes them.

The questions we have been discussing, the questions of Bible and canon, of criticism and authority, are for me ultimately questions of two things: the continuity of theology, and the unity of theology. By continuity I mean this: theology, including biblical scholarship, is a continuous growth. It is not likely that we cut back to, let us say, the Reformation ideals, as if things took a wrong turning after that time, so that we might simply eliminate the Enlightenment and start out on a different road. The Enlightenment took place precisely because these earlier ideals led serious thinkers to it. It is a deeply essential part of our heritage. The world of critical theology, in which free biblical research is an essential part and historical criticism a small but highly symptomatic element, is as much part of our tradition as is the thought of Calvin or the world of the Fathers. Radical attempts to turn the clock back are, indeed, not illegitimate and not impossible, but they are also not likely and not easily to be accepted. If there are to be new developments, and certainly several possibilities now stand before us, such as a greater interest in the canon on one side, a greater possibility of a non-historical exegesis on the other, then these new possibilities are likely to be fruitful only if they take up within themselves the fruits and the insights of the preceding period.

The matter of the unity of theology has been touched on already. Biblical theology in itself can never have the final word in theological decision, and even patterns that are widely accepted as decisive for biblical understanding cannot thereby be taken as absolutes for theology as a whole. Ultimate theological decisions can be attempted and achieved only when all the relevant considerations have been taken into account; and biblical theology as such has never attempted to do that. In the fine words of Sean McEvenue: 'Theological truths are not reached by deduction or dialectic or any form of reasoning restricted to the canon or a deposit of faith. They are determined in judgements which have reflected on what scripture says and also on whatever other clearly relevant knowledge the theologian may possess. There is no single point of departure and no single final norm. Theological truths are discovered by open minds passionately hungry for contemporary, true understanding of God.'[19] One of the reasons for this takes us back to the beginning of our discussion: faith is not derived from scripture, but scripture is derived from faith. Scripture was, in the end, very properly bounded by the presence of a canon; one can hardly see how it could have been left otherwise. But the canon is not very important. Scripture itself in its content makes it clear to us that the boundary of the canon does not necessarily or always express precisely the horizon of authority in Christian believing.

[19] *Interpretation* 35, 1981, 236–7.

Some passages relevant to the formation of the canon

1. Order of books in the Hebrew Bible as commonly printed:
   a. Torah: Genesis, Exodus, Leviticus, Numbers, Deuteronomy
   b. Prophets: i. 'Former': Joshua, Judges, Samuel, Kings
        ii. 'Latter': Isaiah, Jeremiah, Ezekiel and the twelve Minor Prophets (Hosea, Joel, Amos, Obadiah, Jonah, Micah, Nahum, Habakkuk, Zephaniah, Haggai, Zechariah, Malachi)
   c. Writings: Psalms, Job, Proverbs, the Five Megilloth or Scrolls (Ruth, Song of Songs, Ecclesiastes, Lamentations, Esther), Daniel, Ezra, Nehemiah, Chronicles

   This is the order of the standard printed edition *Biblia Hebraica Stuttgartensia* (*BHS*). In the Writings there are often minor variations of order. The Leningrad Manuscript, on which *BHS* is based, begins them with: Chronicles, Psalms, Job, Proverbs. Many editions print Song of Songs before Ruth and Lamentations before Ecclesiastes. But the division between the three major groups is always maintained alike.

2. Order of the books in the Greek Old Testament ('Septuagint') as commonly printed (order as in the edition of Rahlfs):
   Genesis, Exodus, Leviticus, Numbers, Deuteronomy, Joshua, Judges, Ruth, 1–4 Kingdoms (= Samuel and Kings), Paralipomena (= Chronicles), 1 Ezra (not in Hebrew canon), 2 Ezra (= Ezra and Nehemiah of Hebrew canon), Esther, Judith, Tobit, 1–4 Maccabees, Psalms, Odes (= various poems from scripture), Proverbs, Ecclesiastes, Song of Songs, Job, Wisdom, Ecclesiasticus (= Ben Sira), Psalms of Solomon, Twelve Minor Prophets, Isaiah, Jeremiah + Baruch + Lamentations + Letter of Jeremiah, Ezekiel, Susanna + Daniel + Bel and the Dragon

3. Passages in Ben Sira (= Ecclesiasticus; early 2nd century BC):
   a. Mention of the 'twelve prophets' (i.e. our 'Minor Prophets') as a group:
     49.10: May the bones of the twelve prophets also send forth new life (NEB)

b. Persons celebrated in the 'praise of famous men', chs. 44–50
(Greek text):
Enoch, Noah, Abraham, Isaac, Jacob, Moses, Aaron,
Phinehas, Joshua, Caleb, the Judges, Samuel, Nathan,
David, Solomon, Elijah, Elisha, Hezekiah, Isaiah, Josiah,
Jeremiah, Ezekiel, Twelve Prophets, Zerubbabel, Joshua
son of Jozadak, Nehemiah. Enoch, Joseph, Shem, Seth,
Adam. Simon son of Onias the high priest.

c. From the prologue of the Greek translator (later 2nd
century BC):

> A legacy of great value has come to us through the law,
> the prophets, and the writers who followed in their
> steps... [After apologizing for possible defects in the
> translation] but works do not have the same force when
> spoken in their own Hebrew and when they are
> translated into another language. Not only this, but also
> the Law itself and the Prophets and the rest of the books
> have no small difference when read in the original.

4. Josephus against Apion, i. 37–42 (around 100 AD):

(Unlike the Greeks) we (Jews) do not have myriads of
inconsistent and conflicting books, but only *twenty-two*, which
are justly accredited and contain the record of all time.

Of these, five are the books of Moses, comprising the laws
and the traditional history from the origin of man down to the
death of the lawgiver. This period falls just short of three
thousand years. From the death of Moses until Artaxerxes,
who succeeded Xerxes as king of Persia, the prophets
subsequent to Moses wrote the history of the events of their
own times in thirteen books. The remaining books contain
hymns to God and precepts for the conduct of human life.
From Artaxerxes to our own time the complete history has
been written, but has not been deemed worthy of equal credit
with the earlier records, because there has not been the exact
succession of the prophets...

Although long ages have now passed, no one has dared to
add, to remove or to replace anything; it is an instinct with
every Jew from the day of his birth to regard them as the
decrees of God, to abide by them and if necessary cheerfully to
die for them.

(Translation follows Thackeray)

5. Probable reconstruction of Josephus's scheme of twenty-two:
   a. Pentateuch   5
   b. Joshua; Judges + Ruth; Samuel; Kings;
      Isaiah; Jeremiah + Lamentations; Ezekiel;
      Twelve Minor Prophets; Job; Daniel; Ezra-
      Nehemiah; Chronicles; Esther   13
   c. Psalms; Proverbs; Ecclesiastes;
      Song of Songs   4
                                                                  ___
                                                                   22

6. Fourth Ezra 14.37ff. (cf. R.H. Charles, *Pseudepigrapha*, pp. 623f.):

   [The Law is burnt and lost, and must be restored]—So I [Ezra] took five men... The Most High gave understanding to the five men, and they wrote what was dictated in order, in characters which they knew not. They sat forty days; they wrote in the daytime and at night they did eat bread... In forty days were written ninety-four books. And it came to pass when the forty days were fulfilled, that the Most High spoke to me saying: Publish the twenty-four books that you have written, that the worthy and the unworthy may read (in them); but the seventy you shall keep, to deliver them to the wise among your people.

Further Thoughts on Canonical Criticism

1. *General.* Reference has been made again and again in the above chapters to various tendencies of modern canonical criticism; but these were not fully documented or discussed with reference to actual books and discussions. This appendix is intended to gather together a number of the more technical and specialized points, and some closer arguments about the books on the subject, which might otherwise have burdened the argument of the preceding chapters. I hope readers will forgive me if I begin in a somewhat autobiographical style; but it seems to me that in the entire discussion very much depends upon the way in which one sees the scholarly scene in which one works, and the way in which it has developed. If I differ from much that has been said by the authors of modern canonical criticism, one main reason is that I perceive the scholarly scene in at least Old Testament and theology in a quite different way from that in which they do. The simplest way to express this seems to be in personal terms.

I was myself never much of a historical-critical scholar. I do not know that I ever detected a gloss, identified a source, proposed an emendation or assigned a date. If scholarship is as much dominated by historical criticism as we nowadays hear, such a record must be rare. But of course it is not. Professor Childs warns us (*JSOT* 16, 1980, 59) not 'simply to assume the validity of the older critical model in which we have all been trained'. He must speak for himself. I would not say that I was so 'trained'. What many or most of my generation of Old Testament scholars were trained in was the atmosphere of the biblical theology movement, which Childs has described and analysed so well. Although in that movement traditional historical criticism was recognized as legitimate (as it is by Childs) and indeed as exegetically relevant (as by him for the most part it is not), very few people supposed that the separation of sources, the dating of books and the like was the cutting edge of scholarship or that it was the essential and decisive step in the achieving of a theological interpretation. On the contrary, scholars who thought that these matters were the essence of exegesis and that after them little more need be done were rather laughed at and looked upon as fossils from some earlier age. The cutting edge of Old Testament study, and its impact upon theology, seemed to lie rather in the concepts of biblical theology. This movement was interested in the special character of the Bible, its difference from any other literature or system of thought, its relation to the church and its proclamation, the unity of the Bible and the relation of the Old Testament to the New, and its place in the witness of the church. On the one hand many of these questions seemed to be little helped forward by traditional biblical criticism: it could, for instance, hardly tell one how the Old Testament differed from mythological polytheism, or how it was related to the New Testament. On the other hand differing historical and critical positions seemed not to make very much difference to the theological evaluation: so long as it was a work of biblical theology, a work that considered Deutero-Isaiah as exilic and one that considered it as post-exilic could be used together without any too great conflict, and likewise one that (like the older critical positions) considered most of Ezekiel to be the work of that prophet and one that considered him to have composed only a handful of verses. Within biblical theology such questions no longer seemed to be so decisive. Historical criticism, although accepted, was not very important. There was, indeed, within biblical theology considerable common ground with many who did not even accept it. Abundant evidence of that climate of theological opinion exists in the books and articles of the period 1945–60 or 1940–65. That was the climate in which I and many others were 'trained'. In just that atmosphere, as it was round about 1948–50, a position like that now taken by Childs would have fitted in very well with the setting of my own mind.

A position like that of canonical criticism therefore, far from being novel, seems to me to be very much *déjà vu*. Far from being a quite new solution to problems that have been overwhelming us, it seems to me to be a reiteration in rather different terms of the sort of position from which I for one found it necessary to depart, and its strong opposition to the relevance of historical criticism is a solution to a problem which for a long time has been known not to be a very serious one. In particular, it is important to observe that opposition to the claims of canonical criticism is not necessarily, and often not in fact, based on the assumption of 'the validity of the older critical model'.

My own response to the development of the movement, until the appearance of Childs's *Introduction*, was cautiously favourable throughout. My 1974 article[1] expresses considerable sympathy with the general approach, including the interest in canonicity and in the final form of the text, as well as in the positive relations to

---

[1] 'Trends and Prospects in Biblical Theology', *JTS* 25, 1974, 273–4.

pre-modern exegesis; but it expressed doubts about the absolutiza-
tion of the canon as an exegetical principle, and indicated that the
canon was one thing and the final form of books something
different. This was written on the basis of Childs's *Biblical Theology
in Crisis* (1970), the only work in the series I had then seen. My
Chicago lecture of 1975[2] says that 'the explication of the story itself,
as a story, is the right form for a biblical theology' and goes on to
say that 'this is an important element in the programme of Childs to
which we can entirely assent'; but it also qualifies this assent, in that
Childs unduly limits this by expressing it in terms of the *canon* and
suggesting that this is the one and only method for biblical theology.
My article in the *Interpreter's Dictionary of the Bible*, Supplementary volume (1976), pp. 110–11, makes a similar assessment but is
by no means negative towards Childs's proposals. In my article on
'Historical Reading', given as a lecture in 1978 and now having as
reference Childs's Göttingen lecture delivered in that same year, I
wrote favourably about his view of Deutero-Isaiah and the change
in the level of meaning effected by incorporation within the book as
a whole, argued that this 'shows up a defect in the critical approach
as it has been generally practised', and pointed to the excessive
concentration of traditional criticism upon the 'original', suggesting
that the emphasis should now move towards the understanding of
effects rather than of origins.[3]

All of this indicates a rather sympathetic position towards the
direction in which canonical criticism then appeared to be going. In
none of these statements did I express fears that traditional
historical criticism would be threatened by the new proposals, nor
did I suggest that historical criticism was the touchstone by which
their validity should be tested. As a matter of fact, these writings
contain passages which explore with some sympathy the possibilities of a quite non-historical interpretation.

The effect of Childs's *Introduction* was to convince me that the
programme of canonical criticism was essentially confused and self-
contradictory in its conceptual formulation. In so far as this arises
from its attitude to historical criticism, my resistance to its claims is
not based on the fact that it seems opposed to historical criticism,
and I never suggested this. Rather, it would lie in the following
three points: 1. Canonical criticism, as it turns out, is in large
measure not different in its framework and methods from scholarship informed by historical criticism; its difference lies in the

[2] *Explorations in Theology 7*, p. 16 and pp. 144f., n. 33 = *Journal of Religion* 56, 1976,
p. 16 and n. 32.
[3] *Explorations in Theology 7*, pp. 46f.

periods and aspects upon which it focuses. The strong antipathy shown to traditional criticism by Childs therefore constitutes a contradiction within his entire operation. 2. Childs's attacks on previous scholarship may or may not be justified in themselves, but in the context of his book they often represent the only specific and evidenced argumentation for his case. As I wrote in my *JSOT* article, 'the demonstration of the case comes to be excessively dependent on one particular element, namely the contrast between the weaknesses and antinomies of historical criticism on the one hand and the virtues of the canonical reading on the other'. These weaknesses and antinomies, even if they are real, are simply no ground for reasoning to the sort of picture of canon and theology which Childs proposes. His case was stronger and more attractive when presented without this argument. Since his theological views are in any case disputable, and since his actual view of the canon and its shape is rather weak, his book sometimes gives the impression that the dismantling of scholarship and its reconstitution under new principles is his real interest.[4] 3. Childs handles historical criticism not primarily as a question of truth—as far as truth goes he tends to accept it—but as a matter of relevance or appropriateness. This is connected with points discussed elsewhere.[5]

Thus, to sum up this point, historical criticism is an issue in this discussion not because Childs says so many things against it, but because his use of his arguments in this respect reveals deep faults and incoherences in his thinking. It is also an issue because he has greatly exaggerated the dominance of historical criticism in scholarship, considering that in the post-war decades it was of rather limited and muted influence. Indeed, if canonical criticism had continued to be launched as a positive programme, and if the case for it had not been made to depend so much on the antipathy to historical criticism, it is doubtful whether the latter would ever have become an issue in this particular discussion at all.

To approach the matter from another angle, let us go back again to the 'Biblical Theology Movement', which Childs described so well. Apart from certain flaws, his analysis of it seems to me to be very good, and I do not agree that really vital objections were made by those who disliked it.[6] But from the beginning I failed to see any intrinsic connection between Childs's description of that movement

---

[4] Cf. Harrelson in *JBL* 100, 1981, 99–103.
[5] Cf. above, pp. 118f.
[6] E.g. J.D. Smart, *The Past, Present and Future of Biblical Theology* (Philadelphia: Westminster Press, 1979); S. Terrien in *Horizons in Biblical Theology* 3, 1981, 143. Such questions as whether it was really a 'movement', or whether it was really American and not international, seem to me not to matter much.

and its decline in the first part of his book, and the announcement of his own proposal for a canon-centred biblical theology in the latter part of the same book. Only on p. 102 of *Biblical Theology in Crisis* do we suddenly hear that a persistently weak point of biblical theology was 'its failure to take the biblical text seriously in its canonical form'. But the entire excellent exposé of that movement, as given by Childs himself, conspicuously failed to provide evidence to back this assertion. Nowhere did his analysis provide reason to suppose that lack of attention to the *canon* was the specific cause of its problems.

Certainly in the biblical theology of that time the word *canon* was not used every three or four lines; but it seems obvious to me that the canon was by implication very much a central matter. The earnest emphasis of the movement on the unity and distinctiveness of the Bible was an implicit welcome to the idea of the canon as boundary of a highly special area. Theologies of the Old and New Testaments were living celebrations of the fact that the biblical canon, as distinct from most or all that lies outside it, is the locus where the true picture of God and his works is to be found. What was within was (in some way) revelation, what was outside was something very different. A highly influential work like Cullmann's on time was surely an exposition of an implied philosophy which justified the belief that the New Testament books, and these alone, belonged to the time of revelation and thus formed a special group. Biblical theology was very much a canonical movement even if it did not use the word much.

Thus as a matter of pure description Childs's depiction of the movement fails to provide a prolegomenon to justify his own proposals that follow. His proposal, when it comes, comes like a rabbit out of a hat. It could be the answer, but there was nothing in the fate of biblical theology that demonstrated that it was the answer. Many of the central questions of biblical theology can be simply translated into questions about the canon, if one prefers to express them so. Salvation history or revelation in history, for example, were key concepts, and they certainly represented a true reality in the Bible: one could have said the biblical canon displayed them to a unique degree or in a very special way. But, it could be objected, they did not exactly coincide with the boundaries of the Old Testament: there were materials within which did not use these concepts, and there were materials outside which did seem to use them. Salvation history, therefore, though certainly a valid aspect of scripture, did not have boundaries that coincided exactly with the canon as the boundary of scripture. In such respects biblical theology was very much concerned with the canon in its discussions.

Thus canonical criticism, far from being something completely different in character from 'the American Biblical Theology Movement', and far from being a replacement for it after its decline, seems to me much more a new version of it, motivated very largely by the same values. Childs (*Crisis*, p. 102) speaks of the 'shifting winds' that blew through the skies of biblical theology: Cullmann's salvation history, Bultmann's self-understanding, Ebeling and Fuchs's linguisticality. Canonical criticism is another of these shifting winds: its emphasis on the canon, although much more explicit in these terms, seems to me to be just another version of the emphasis on the unique character of the Bible which was central to all currents of the movement. All these 'shifting winds' blew because their authors, like Childs, strongly believed that they had found a principle which was normative and which enabled the Bible to be normative, and they could show, as he does, that there is an aspect of the Bible for which this works. Childs seems to be convinced that the canon is different because it is *de fide*; but of course the canon is not *de fide*, or not in any very important sense. A tried principle of the older biblical theology like salvation history had far greater claims to be *de fide* than the canon has.

The difference can be expressed, perhaps, as a shift from content to form. The older biblical theology sought to find a principle of biblical uniqueness in some aspect of *content*: Hebrew thought, biblical thought, the biblical idea of time, salvation history, the covenant, existential personalism, and so on. None of these seemed to fit perfectly with the exact boundaries of the Bible, and they to some extent conflicted with one another, as well as incurring criticism on the grounds of the doubtful ways in which their own character had been established. Childs was well aware of all these difficulties. There seemed to be no principle of content that was reliably worked out and that coincided exactly with the needed normativeness of the Bible. The canon answered this problem. By its own nature it coincided exactly with the boundary of scripture. It was a formal principle rather than one of content. By taking the canon as principle one was no longer forced to argue that there was an absolute difference in content, in ideas, in thought patterns, between the Bible and the rest of the world. If there was common conceptual material between the Bible and the environing world, this need no longer matter: the biblical material was normative, not because it was necessarily different in content, but because the canon separated it off and gave it its distinctive shape. The element of comparativism, which the older biblical theology felt as a much more serious threat than historical criticism, might thus be neutralized, for comparative similarities could be freely accepted without endangering the special status of scripture. This aspect was a very promising one and stimulated much of my own original favourable reaction to the nascent canonical approach.

Moreover, the canon, because it was a formal principle, seemed to be beyond argument. Childs was much exercised by the fact that biblical theology could not achieve hermeneutical *certainty* (*Crisis*, p. 102): of the various interpretative guides that were offered, many were disputable, and some disagreed with others. It was not certain that they agreed in fact with scripture, not in all its dimensions. But no one could doubt that the canon agreed with the dimensions and the boundaries of scripture, for it by its own nature *was* these dimensions and boundaries. As a hermeneutical guide it was by definition infallible. The canon was the Grail for which the American Biblical Theology Movement had been the Quest.

This need not have been surprising, since that movement, as I have argued, had implicitly been very canonically-minded all along; the difference lay in the fact that the canon principle was now fully formulated, and the statement of it could demarcate it more exactly and finally from all other approaches. Since no other principle could possibly compete with the canon in the perfection of its coincidence with the boundaries of scripture, it followed that all other possible principles took some kind of 'vantage point outside the text' (*Crisis*, p. 102) and were therefore bound to be in greater or lesser degree wrong.

Canonical criticism thus completes the quest of the Biblical Theology Movement. The canon principle makes explicit the special and unique normativity of the Bible, which that movement had sought to establish all along. The threat presented by comparativism has been neutralized, even if only externally and artificially (the canon principle makes it unnecessary even to bother with looking at the evidence of Canaanite parallels, Greek mystery cults and the like: their evidence, whether strong or weak, becomes automatically irrelevant). Historical criticism, as already remarked, though legitimate, presents no way forward towards theological understanding. It is not a positively important matter for theology. Childs (*JSOT*, 16, 1980, 59) thinks that it would be good if the perception of scholarship as 'liberal' and 'conservative' could be overcome. Exactly the same aspiration was being expressed by scholars of the older biblical theology, like George Ernest Wright, thirty years earlier.

Above all, however, canonical criticism in Childs's form of it continues the older tradition in that it believes in biblical theology at all. Why should there be a 'biblical' theology at all and what content could such a theology have? Moreover, in what sense could it be described as truly 'theological'? The answer had been that there was some sort of distinctive content of biblical thought, which was different from the data unearthed by criticism and comparative study, but also different from the thinking of modern dogmatic theology: these differences and this content constituted the legitimacy and the subject matter of biblical theology. Biblical theology was thus a matter of content, as anything worthy of the name of 'theology' must be. In offering an answer in terms not of content but of form, i.e. of canon, Childs failed to face the most obvious conclusion: namely, that there was no room for any biblical theology at all. For theology is a matter of content. Even if scripture is the sole source for theology and the canon the sole guide to its interpretation, theology cannot merely describe the shape of the canon: it must say something about God, about his works, about Christ and salvation. But in order to do this it must take up just that which Childs forbids, a 'vantage point outside the text'; for only so is it in a position to make estimative judgements, to make decisions about truth. (Or are we to be forbidden to make any such judgements?) There was good reason, on the basis of Childs's own depiction of biblical theology, to come to the conclusion that no such subject was viable. The movement, as he had argued, had largely collapsed; extremely acute theologians like Gilkey had drawn the moral that there could never be any biblical theology anyway; and there were good reasons, even from within biblical theology, and even as Childs himself depicted it (e.g. *Crisis*, p. 83), for seeing the possibilities of biblical theology as no more than preparatory, tentative suggestions, the full explication of which must await a 'dialogue' between biblical and dogmatic theologians. In another words, biblical theology at the best could never hope to decide anything that was really theological—exactly my own view. But, if this was so, there was no point in announcing a new programme of canonical criticism on the ground that it was the way to realizing a 'new biblical theology'. The reasons Childs urges for such an aim, in his chapter on 'the Need for a New Biblical Theology' (*Crisis*, pp. 91-6), are really utilitarian—pastors need to have such a biblical theology. But, whether pastors need it or not, they cannot have it if the principles laid down prevent it. In fact what the principles of canonical criticism suggest is something different: a canon-conscious exegesis, not a biblical theology but a theologically conscious reflection on the individual texts. To this one might add a description of the contours of the canon, but a description is what it would be; yet 'description' was one of the bad words of most biblical theology. Canonical criticism, then, leads away from any reality of biblical theology: to regard it as if it was the gateway to a new biblical theology was surely a sign that the values of that older movement still survived. Its assumptions had not been rethought, but only translated into other words.

To sum up, in canonical criticism we may see a line of thought in which those elements of the older biblical theology which ran into the greater trouble, such as Hebrew thought or salvation history, are stripped away or neutralized, but many of the other outlooks of the movement remain unchanged, the canon itself being a central example: the anti-historicism, the diagnosis of historical study as objectivist in its ideals, the anti-objectivism, the distrust of specialized expertise, the desire to prevent the subject from being drawn apart by different disciplines and the need to find a way to see it visibly as a whole—all of these were entirely normal already in the forties.

There were indeed several changes of scene which took place between the time of the older biblical theology and the newer realization of the same movement in canonical criticism. The first was the enormous growth of generally 'structuralist' ideas about language, literature, and understanding, which made it possible to reduce the older emphasis on history and to put in its place a greater stress upon synchronic interpretation. The second was the great revival of interest in all the comparativist, philological, and historical areas, on the edge of the Bible, which the biblical theology movement had sought to damp down. Ugarit, Qumran, and Nag Hammadi all immensely reinforced the importance of expert knowledge of the background in which the Bible had been formed. On the American scene the phenomenon of Albright and the Albrightian school was particularly prominent. Hardly to be labelled 'historical-critical', and perhaps something more like 'historical-speculative', this school had a certain footing within biblical theology; but, on the other hand, it tended on the whole to suggest that questions of biblical exegesis could be decided, or had been decided, by the evidence of Canaanite inscriptions recently discovered or by theoretical reconstructions of ancient Hebrew orthography. Thus knowledge from outside the biblical world seemed to be taken to decide the meaning and interpretation of things within that world. It is probable that antipathy to these pretensions (if they were such) of the Albright school is an important ingredient in the generation of canonical criticism. It was here, if anywhere, that claims to an inductive, scientific, objective procedure may have circulated—ideas that were later to be projected upon the historical-critical enterprise (the Albright school, though accepting some elements of traditional historical criticism, leant in fact in a heavily conservative direction, speculating as freely in the direction of early dates and extreme reliability as other critics were supposed to have speculated in the direction of late dates and unreliability). It is doubtful whether the strong devaluation of alternative types of criticism by the canonical critics would have taken place but for the powerful recent influence of the Albrightians on the American scene. Thirdly, the traditional questions of historical criticism, which had been muted and subdued in the older period of biblical theology, resurfaced in very lively forms. If this upset the received results of historical criticism, it also made the subject much more lively and interesting. If Rendtorff questioned the traditional position in Pentateuchal analysis, Van Seters brought down the Abraham traditions to the exilic or post-exilic age. While the older biblical theology had been able to rest upon the general consensus of earlier historical criticism, without attaching very much importance to it, movements of such drastic character were likely to have a considerable, and unpredictable, effect on even theological exegesis. Of these three factors, the second and the third may well have emphasized the importance of reaching a position about the Bible which would be isolated from the effect of these external and changeable currents of opinion, while the first confirmed that such a position was possible. The *motivations* of canonical criticism, however, remain very much those of the older biblical theology.

2. *Form criticism.* Another way in which we may understand the development of canonical criticism is this: it comes from people whose background lies particularly in the combination of form criticism and hermeneutics. In America the two were particularly closely associated. Childs himself notes the affinity to form criticism: defending his conception (*JSOT* 16, 1980, 52), he writes: 'In one sense, I have simply extended the insights of the form critical method.' That this is so is evident to the informed reader. But to 'simply extend' the insights of this method is a very dubious basis for justification. What it seems to mean is: form criticism worked with short and limited units, it sought to identify their situation in life, and it supposed that the form of units would thus reveal their purpose. It was thus not an unnatural idea to extend this, so that the unit would not be a short poem or group of laws but the Bible as a whole: the entire Bible is the 'form' which is to be understood. Form criticism, suitably extended, will yield a method by which the canonical form will tell us what is the purpose of the canonical whole. Not an unnatural extension, but a rather unthinking one. For, firstly, what is valid for small units cannot necessarily be applied to large units. Many disciplines are aware that differences of scale must require different methods of treatment. Secondly, form criticism—as it has been understood in

biblical scholarship—seems to me to be one of the most unverified and precarious of all the critical approaches. Compared with (say) traditional historical criticism, which sets off the texts against some sort of external scale, such as the history of Israel's religion, form criticism has often been very speculative. When one considers the many strong criticisms which Childs levels against numerous forms of traditional biblical criticism, it seems to me extraordinary that form criticism of all things should be taken as a basis for the justification of anything. If critical methods need to be thoroughly rethought—and why not?—form criticism would be an ideal point at which to begin.

3. *Barth.* It is also interesting to consider the relation of the programme of canonical criticism to Barth; many reviewers of Childs's work have asked questions about this. We may begin by going back to *Crisis*, p. 111, where Childs tells us that Barth worked 'from an avowed theological context, namely, from the context of the Christian canon'; he thinks I had failed to realize that this was the true basis of what I had called Barth's 'alienation from the world of biblical scholarship'. But Childs is quite wrong here: this is not a true representation of Barth. The matter of the canon was not so very important for him, and the word 'canon' is not found on every third or fourth line of his enormous *Dogmatics*. Childs is reading into Barth his own canonical interest. Barth's difference from biblical scholarship lay in fact on a different plane and applied in cases where there was no question either about the canon or about historical criticism. His position was most clearly seen in the interpretation of St. Paul, in which differences about canon and about critical matters were of rather limited force. His basic stance was the extrinsic character of interpretation. The meaning of the text lay not in the mind or the intention of Paul but in the extrinsic realities, the theological real world, to which this pointed. Interpretation depended on this extrinsic reality and not on intentionality and the like. This meant that only an interpretation on the level of dogmatic theology could do justice to the texts.

In this respect Childs's approach stands on the side of traditional biblical scholarship and not on the side of Barth. The contours of meaning are to be drawn not by the extrinsic realities but by the lines of shape of the canon itself. Interpretation is decided in canonical criticism not by the theological realities, by the nature of God, of Christ, of salvation, but by the mind of the writer, like the mind of Paul: the writer is a curiously anonymous and composite person, the canon and the canonizers, but functions in that same way: the idea that the canon has 'intentionality' is a striking betrayal of this.

Another aspect lies in the concept of biblical theology. Childs, outlining his programme (*Crisis*, p. 110), tells us that Barth 'remained invulnerable to the weaknesses of the biblical theology movement'. He had 'nothing to do with' *Heilsgeschichte* (this was certainly an exaggeration: Barth had much more to do with salvation history than he had with the canon), Hebrew mentality, or unity in diversity of the Bible (this last again an exaggeration, for Barth certainly came close to this). Therefore, Childs thinks, the work of historical critics was only a prolegomenon to real exegesis. But the purport of all this is misread by Childs. Certainly Barth thought most contemporary biblical scholarship to be only preparatory to exegesis; but then he would probably have said the same of biblical theology as a whole; and for a special programme for biblical theology, to which Childs dedicates himself with so much fervour, he would have had no more room than for salvation history. If Barth was invulnerable to the weaknesses of biblical theology, which I think to be a partially true judgement, it was largely because to him biblical theology, as something different from dogmatics, did not matter very much. Thus Childs's idea that it is a matter of great importance to develop a *biblical* theology on the basis of the canon has nothing much to do with Barth's mind. Barth could get the results he needed without worrying much about the canon, because he approached them from the other side, from the side of what God in revelation was really like. It is because it is planned as a *biblical* theology, as one depending on the contours of biblical evidence and working from that side, that the emphasis on the canon in Childs's conception has to be so great. Barth might, of course, have liked canonical criticism: in general, he liked things more if they were more 'theological', and thus for example he thought it significant that a 'theological' dictionary of the New Testament was being prepared. This does not alter the fact that canonical criticism as now practised is quite far from Barth, and is as much against his mind as according to it.

The fact is that if Barth's general lines of thinking are to be moved from the dogmatic level and restated on the level of any sort of biblical theology, something has to be modified. *No* biblical theology has the means to agree entirely with Barth, unless it simply becomes subservient to his dogmatics. This is true for the reason already given, namely that all biblical theology can be only partial, tentative, and preparatory: theological decisions in the ultimate sense can be taken only when *all* the relevant considerations are taken into account. This is true not only of Barth, but of other major theologians; but Barth is a case very much in point, because he has been particularly influential upon biblical theology.

As already stated, Barth was very insistent on exegesis in terms of the extrinsic referents, the theological realities to which the text 'pointed'. This was extremely important for him. Thus—if one was to have a biblical theology at all—one concentrated on events in history, as expressed for instance by G. Ernest Wright, was very much in the spirit of Barth, and was very welcome at the time in circles that venerated Barth. Eventually Wright came to think that he was very much against Barth, but in that earlier and creative period of biblical theology there was a good deal of similarity. Only very gradually did it become plain that for Wright the history in question was very much empirical history, moved by historical forces and verifiable by archaeological investigation. This would not have been welcome to Barth or his more slavish followers. Yet it is one of the intelligible ways in which one may go, starting from Barth. If revelation lies in historical events extrinsic to the text, to which the text witnesses, then in the last resort there is an equivocation if the events are not in principle subject to some sort of empirical verification, or unless an explanation is given why they are not. It is exactly this side which was expanded by Pannenberg's theology, which was of course very welcome to Wright in his later years. The point of this is as follows: the emphasis on the canon in canonical criticism does not seem to be to be any more true to the heritage of Barth than was (say) Wright's version of salvation history, or many other solutions of the older biblical theology.

We shall come back to Barth again in a moment, but first we may consider the relations to:

4. *Bultmann and Hermeneutics.* Canonical criticism appears to have more affinity in many ways with the wave of interest in hermeneutics which was felt in the United States in the earlier sixties. Hermeneutics, as thus understood, laid great emphasis on the present-day appropriation of material. Much depended on the standpoint of the interpreter. Even if it was known what was the meaning for the original author and for his audience, the question remained, what was the meaning for today, and what elements in the original complex of meaning were still relevant? This approach was anti-objectivist and anti-historicist, in this respect only reinforcing the mixture of these two strains which had been common in the biblical theology movement from the beginning. According to this point of view, the historically known meaning could not and should not be objectivized as if it was *the true* meaning; and, conversely, historical study did not provide objective knowledge of a matter: rather, the historian himself was enmeshed in the quest for present-day meaning and his decisions were a distillate from that quest. Historical knowledge was relative to the situation and the problems

of the modern interpreter. And in particular, this strain of hermeneutics emphasized the difference in principle between the perceptions attained by the natural sciences and those attained by the human sciences. It tended to paint traditional historical study in positivist colours, as if it had taken the natural sciences as its model; and this diagnosis of the problem, though clearly contrary to a mass of facts in the modern writing of history, was widely accepted in theological circles. Traditional historical work, including biblical criticism, came to be seen as if it had been positivistic in character; and the claim that it failed to deliver the goods in the form of interpretation for the needs of the present day was redoubled.

This current of hermeneutical thinking, however, was full of contradictions as it worked out in the theology of the English-speaking countries. It was introduced into the United States primarily as the means of inaugurating a 'New Quest of the Historical Jesus'; the old quest had gone wrong because it stuck to the older ideals of history, the new ideas of hermeneutic historiography would enable the question to be taken up in a new way. In fact it is doubtful whether a single inch of progress was made: no more seems to be known about the historical Jesus than before the New Quest was launched, and even the subject of the New Quest is little talked about. This conspicuous lack of success did not prevent a wide influence of the ideas of this sort of hermeneutic from taking place.

Most workers in the older biblical theology had some degree of agreement with Barth and also some with Bultmann. It was through Bultmann's influence, however, that this hermeneutical current came to be known. But this was the cause of serious tension with the more Barthian side. Barth in particular had been vehement in his warnings against the acceptance of a basis for interpretation in natural theology or in philosophy. The whole idea of a 'biblical theology' depended on general agreement with him in this respect: biblical theology was something that could be and should be worked out separately from any particular philosophy. But the hermeneutics introduced in the wake of Bultmann depended explicitly not only on philosophy but on one particular philosophy. Yet there was comparatively little objection to them on this ground. Moreover, not only did this hermeneutic depend on a particular philosophy, there was good reason to suppose that that particular philosophy was a wrong one. It was probably wrong in one of its deepest convictions, namely that of the fundamental difference of principle between the natural and the human sciences. If this was wrong, then the practical consequences would be wrong also. It is possible to argue that the truth conditions applicable in the humanities are not in essence different from those applicable in the sciences, even if the kinds of complexity and of structure differ greatly. Moreover, and particularly in the United States, the modern world displays the importance of social sciences, which may perhaps enjoy a position somewhere between those of the traditional humanities and of the traditional sciences. It was, as we have seen, from some of these newer disciplines, such as linguistics, that the newer and less historical approaches had actually evolved, approaches which had favoured movements like the rise of canonical criticism. All in all, therefore, it was strange that not only technical groups of theologians but also large strata of the clergy should allow themselves to accept this sort of philosophical basis as if it was almost authoritative.

In this hermeneutic the aspect of relevance was much stressed. But in the United States relevance easily deteriorated into utility. Part of the excitement about hermeneutics itself was surely inspired by the motive of utility: it was thought that hermeneutics would lead into a method that could then provide a practical guide. More serious is the effect on knowledge: if a certain type of knowledge is considered not to be 'relevant' for a certain purpose, this is commonly construed as if it means that that knowledge is not useful and that one would for practical purposes be better not to know about it at all. None of this, needless to say, would have been accepted by the learned German thinkers from whom the whole system of thought derived.

This particular hermeneutic current had derived from rather 'radical' types of theological thinking: it was associated, for instance, with the discussion over demythologization. Like a number of other features which contributed to biblical theology, however, this sort of hermeneutic began to be used on the English-speaking theological scene in a very conservative way. It enabled people to think that biblical criticism and other traditional scholarship, though doubtless theoretically legitimate, could simply be ruled out as irrelevant. The real questions to be put to the texts were the questions as modern persons, religiously interested, would put them, and the approach to them depended on the needs of these people, as guided, of course, by conservative religious perspectives. Here was another contradiction: for conservatism may have a good *raison d'être* in that it acts as a barrier against untried modern innovation. But in espousing the 'New Hermeneutic' it abandons that function, for there is no more untried and unconservative position than it.[7] The whole matter is probably a symptom of a

---

[7] Cf. *Explorations in Theology* 7, p. 86.

move, in the more intelligent sectors of conservatism, away from the quotation of biblical evidence and towards hermeneutic theories and questions of interpretation for today. In any case this recent conservative twist in the use of hermeneutical ideas is a significant aspect of our theme.

It is ironic how much of this hermeneutical thinking was originated by Bultmann or transmitted by him. If hermeneutics are so good, we ought to have more scholars like Bultmann. In fact, of course, the current of hermeneutical thinking is being so applied as to discourage the existence of anyone like him. Bultmann as a biblical scholar was all that recent hermeneutical thinking wants to prevent. He was a highly critical scholar, who cut up a work like St. John's Gospel into innumerable sources, sections, glosses, and redactional additions; he was strongly committed to historical investigation; he was, among modern scholars, one of the most deeply related to the history-of-religions approach, and thought it obvious that parallels with Greek mysteries or with Gnosticism were vitally important for the understanding of early Christianity; he had no great interest in the canon, and he made many rather negative statements about the place of the Old Testament within Christianity. A hermeneutical approach emanating from such a man must surely be suspect, and should be rejected by good, canonically-thinking people. Or, if his hermeneutical approach is so good, then we ought to have more scholars like Bultmann, deeply historical-critical and strongly motivated by the parallels known through history of religions. Bultmann would have been disgusted by the utilitarian contempt for historical knowledge, by the Philistine ignoring of religious parallels as irrelevant, that took place in the name of his hermeneutical ideas. The whole matter was deeply self-contradictory.

One of the roots of canonical criticism, as has been suggested above, is the longing for hermeneutical certainty—a longing made not unnatural by the frenetic and contradictory character of the whole discussion about biblical hermeneutics in the sixties. Childs (*Crisis*, p. 102) speaks with intensity of the 'hermeneutical uncertainty' that was suffered by the Biblical Theology Movement. The idea that the canon is the proper context is set forth 'in conscious opposition to this approach to hermeneutics'. It will, in other words, remove all uncertainty about the vantage point from which the biblical material is to be viewed. 'The confession of a canon holds this context [i.e. the context of the canon as the given context for biblical theology] to be normative for the Christian faith.'

This is important, I believe, for the ethos of canonical criticism as it has developed. The canon gives not only relevance, but also certainty. Any doubt about the centrality of the canon, any suggestion that canonical understanding might have to share its influence with some other sort of understanding or might be modified by other forces, must therefore be rejected. Certitude comes from the canon alone. There is no room, therefore, for any compromise: canonical criticism must be the sole controlling force, and it cannot share its dominion with any other way of viewing scripture.

5. *Barth again.* This brings us back to Barth. Though canonical criticism in some of its forms makes a certain appeal to Barth, we have seen that in important regards it also departs from Barth. But the considerations just mentioned bring us back to certain respects in which again it has similarities with Barth.

The first of these respects is its compulsive, as it seems, need to control, to dominate, to be the sole final determinator, and its corresponding inability to accept that its guidance might be modified or complemented by any other method or approach. This appears repeatedly. For example, the interest in the way in which the books, in the hands of their final redactors, approached their final form: is this not akin to the field of the already well-established discipline of redaction criticism? Of course it is. It is in fact exactly the same thing. But canonical critics, or some of them, will not accept this, for it might suggest that canonical criticism is only one among the numerous various kinds of criticism (form criticism, source criticism, textual criticism, etc.); for them it is not one among several, but *the one*, something that unlike all the others provides the essential hermeneutical key; and it must not be seen to derive, as these others do, from the set of traditional critical disciplines, rather it must be seen as something quite apart. Even to call it 'canonical criticism' seems therefore to be a depreciation, as if it was merely one among the various critical methods, when in fact it is (allegedly) a quite new, quite different and quite sovereign approach to all the problems of scripture.

The effect of this exalted status, secondly, is that canonical criticism makes itself unable to discuss on equal terms with any other position. This again is very like Barth. There is no longer any common basis for discussion with contrary positions. Words are no longer to be used in a sense which could provide a common platform with agreed values for contrary views. Rather, they are redefined so that their 'new' meanings lead inevitably to the conclusion that canonical criticism is right. As Childs says,[8] 'some of the misunderstanding of parts of my book stem from replacing my

[8] Childs, *JSOT* 16, 1980, 53.

broad use of the term [canon] with a much narrower, traditional usage, and thus missing the force of the argument'. But the new 'broad' use of the term has a very simple value: its meaning is identical with the proposition 'Childs is right'. If, however, one considers that the new broad usage of the term is a result of confusion in Childs's thinking, then of course one cannot express oneself properly in that new broad usage. In other words, the 'new' terminology is a terminology which will lead inevitably to the solutions preferred by canonical criticism and will make equal and level discussions with other positions difficult. Thus terminology is no accidental factor in the question. The endless repetition of the word 'canon' in canonical criticism is not accident, but necessity: for, as seen from without, the continual reuse of this word is necessary in order to hold together sets of arguments which otherwise would fall apart.

Thus, even if one agrees with the main direction of Childs's thinking, his presentation of it is overwhelmingly *declarative*: it suggests that simple *assertion* of the centrality of the canon constitutes demonstration, that mere *claims* to be a theological method make it so. By contrast with the strength of assertions, the actual reasons offered are often weak. To suppose that the asking for *reasons* for the claims of canonical criticism constitutes a case of the debate between reason and faith[9] is a monumental example. Just *saying* that the canon is central does not make it a matter of faith. Even Wittgenstein[10] thought that one might need to have reasons for what one says.

6. *Conservatism and fundamentalism.* In this respect also the passage of several decades has made much difference to the prospects of biblical theology. As already mentioned, biblical theology often aspired to furnish a bridge between the traditional 'critical' and the traditional 'conservative' positions.[11] There were moments of exaltation in which it believed that it had finally overcome both liberalism and fundamentalism entirely. Recent experience has shown these hopes to be unjustified. Fundamentalism has continued, or revived, with extreme strength: if at one end of the scale it has more intellectual backing and force, at the other end its crude extremism and know-nothingism have been shown in a light more lurid than that of the twenties. The movement of biblical theology seems in this respect to have made little difference. Fundamentalists were able either to ignore it or to absorb it within their own belief system.

[9] Childs in *JSOT* 16, 1980, 56.
[10] Cf. ibid., p. 52. [11] Cf. above, p. 136.

Contrary to some impressions,[12] I never suggested that canonical criticism in Childs's form of it betrayed fundamentalist or conservative tendencies. I stated clearly that his approach was 'clearly non-conservative', and that the conservative/fundamentalist approach was 'not at all Childs's own approach'; and in respect of his dependence on critical results as his starting-point I wrote that 'the author remains entirely a child of the critical movement'.[13] I made it clear that, if conservative opinion welcomes his position, it will be by reading into it its own convictions. At least as far as the traditional parameters of the question go, the views of Childs are built upon what conservatives would regard as a 'liberal' view of scripture.

This does not alter the fact that Childs's valuation of traditional critical scholarship is almost exactly the same as the valuation attached to it by conservative/fundamentalist circles. This seems to me to be simply a fact. And why should he not say so? It is a perfectly reasonable and intelligible judgement; I don't in the slightest object to his expressing it. The damaging thing that this valuation introduces into Childs's work is the way in which it contradicts his own deep dependence upon the tradition of critical scholarship and his own acceptance of it as his starting point. In this respect his work gives the impression of a fulfilment of an inner death-wish of liberal criticism.

There are, moreover, other sides to this question. One of these is the matter of relevance, already mentioned. The criterion of relevance directs attention away from the *truth* of critical decisions: they may be true, but they do not much matter. For theological and practical purposes they can be largely ignored: indeed it may be better not to know about them at all. The effect of this approach may be to provide an easier conservative option than traditional fundamentalism. One does not need to be a fundamentalist. Biblical criticism is quite legitimate. But it is equally legitimate to ignore it. The true biblical scholarship, which works purely from the canonical shape, can largely by-pass it; and theological and practical applications can do so even more. Unlike fundamentalism, which has at least to face the existence of critical opinions, and has to work out a position in face of them, this newer option can leave these difficulties aside. The opening of this possibility is likely to have a strong pro-conservative effect; it is likely also to be a large factor in attracting people to canonical criticism.

---

[12] E.g. Childs himself in *JSOT* 16, 1980, 58f.; R. Murray in *Heythrop Journal* 22 (1981) 443.
[13] *JSOT* 16, 1980, 15 and 23.

Another aspect may lie in the probable ultimate theological aims of canonical criticism. These have not yet been fully stated and there may be some doubt about the direction in which the movement will go. But it is a reasonable understanding if we consider that it is fundamentally aimed at what I have called critical theology, rather than at traditional critical study of the Bible, which is considered at least legitimate.[14] The impression given by much of the argumentation of canonical criticism is: one can never under any circumstances judge that one portion of scripture is more central or more essential than any other; one can never validly weigh and measure the biblical materials and come to the decision that this part comes closer to the heart of the matter than that. One can never validly say that Amos's own teaching is more significant than the work of later followers added to his book. One can never as a theological matter evaluate Isaiah's teaching for itself, as something separate from the book in which it is enshrined. It is forbidden, in other words, to judge in terms of better and worse between various elements in scripture. Hence the vehement opposition to the idea of a canon within the canon. The canon must be seen only as a whole. The historian, indeed, has a right to differentiate between one source and another as earlier and later; but the theologian has no right to differentiate as between that which is more true and that which is less true to divine actuality or revelation.

Or one can perhaps put it in this way: canonical criticism does not imply a narrow and fixed theology in point of content. It may be quite open-minded: all sorts of possibilities are there, guaranteed by the fact of variety within the canon. But, in order to reach and appreciate this variety, one absolutely must pass through the one narrow door, the canon. To enter by any other way is forbidden. The essential part of theology is in effect the prolegomena, which make it clear that the canon and its shape can alone be decisive. For such a theology the canon principle is the sole essential and unnegotiable content. If such a position is indeed implied, it is, in spite of its apparent openness, deeply restrictive in effect: its essence is the denial of the right of theology to work evaluatively upon the materials of the canon.

It is, as I say, still too soon to say definitely whether the theological effects of canonical criticism will go in this direction; but it is a reasonable supposition. Moreover, it connects with another aspect which has been mentioned.[15] It was never right to categorize

---

[14] Cf. above, p. 121.
[15] Cf. above, pp. 105ff. especially 108.

modern biblical research as 'historical criticism': historical criticism, though very important in its particular effects, is only one aspect of a much wider climate of reading and understanding. Historical criticism has thus often been the surface occasion and issue of the conflict between different modes of reading; but it has been the symptom and the test of a different and much deeper question: on the one hand a whole mode of reading the Bible, which has similar effects even where no historical-critical question is involved, and on the other hand the existence of critical theology. It may be that on these deeper questions canonical criticism is adopting and support-ing a much more conservative stance. If historical criticism, though legitimate, is not very relevant, it may only mean that its legitimacy does not do anything to demonstrate that a theological position is other than conservative. The more important issue for a strongly conservative stand may simply lie elsewhere.

Whatever may be the answer to these rather tentative questions, one other point remains under this head. There are signs that canonical criticism, like most of the older biblical theology movement, thinks of its own views as forming some sort of bridge between 'liberal' and 'conservative' approaches to scripture. Along with this, it may well be thought that it was 'historical criticism' which brought about the deep chasm between the two, and that the new canonical interest will provide common ground upon which they may come closer together. This view must also be considered to be a misunderstanding. The reverse is true. It is certainly the case that historical criticism has been the central evident line of conflict between these two approaches to the Bible. Nevertheless it has been the total field of modern biblical research, including the elements informed by critical insights, that has been the effective common ground over many decades. It is within it that conservative scholars have worked throughout. They have often, indeed, failed to inform their constituency of the fact; but the one world of scholarship, within which critical concepts are at home, and in which historical analysis has had a leading role, has in fact formed such a common field. Non-confessional and religiously neutral organizations such as the Society of Biblical Literature in the United States or the Society for Old Testament Study in Great Britain have rendered enormous services in exactly this way. Groupings like the Albright school were also influential in providing a common working territory for people from highly disparate religious backgrounds. The non-confessional and often non-theological society of aca-demic study has rendered very important services to religion. By contrast, the idea that a more theological and more canon-centred approach would overcome the conflicts of interpretation seems a highly speculative one. For the differences among scholars in respect of the different basic kinds of religion that they observe are considerably more severe and unbridgeable than their differences over matters like biblical history and literature.

7. *Judaism and Christianity*. In this respect, as in a number of others, there is a difference between the aspirations with which canonical criticism was developed and the product as it has emerged. In the earlier works of the series Childs seemed to emphasize the idea that the Old Testament was *Christian* scripture. The aim of his commentary on Exodus was 'to interpret... as canonical scripture within the theological discipline of the Christian church'.[16] That commentary has sections on the treatment of the passages in the New Testament and others that offer 'theological reflection on the text within the context of the Christian canon'.[17] These sections help to make intelligible how traditional Christianity used the Old Testament passages; they give useful insights into the way in which the Christian understanding of them developed. In *Crisis*, p. 110, a welcoming understanding is directed towards Calvin's exegesis, in which the 'literal sense' of the Old Testament is understood to include frequent references to Jesus Christ and the life of the Christian church.[18] He thinks modern scholars have generally failed to understand how this worked. All this side of the evolution of canonical criticism, then, emphasized the distinctively *Christian* explication of the Old Testament. Whether one agrees with this or not, it is a quite consistent and intelligible standpoint.

It is surprising, therefore, when one passes to the *Introduction*, which is much the fullest expression of canonical criticism thus far, to find how little this sort of insight has been developed. The New Testament, in fact, is comparatively little mentioned; even the concluding chapter on 'The Hebrew Scriptures and the Christian Bible' is devoted primarily to the question of the Christian Old Testament and its identity, in view of differing views of its extent and definition. Little or nothing is to be heard of the incarnate Christ as a personality inhabiting the Books of Joshua or of Haggai. The discussion seems to stress the kinship of Judaism and Christianity in that the Old Testament is shared by them both. But this, while true, is of minor significance in comparison with the fact that the Christian canon contains also the New Testament, the content of which creates a great gulf between the two religions. The

[16] *Exodus*, p. xiii.
[17] Ibid., p. xvi.
[18] Cf. also McEvenue, *Interpretation* 35, 1981, 233, who, however, seems not to notice the point here being made, namely that these Christological perspectives seem to disappear in the *Introduction*.

canon, far from being a bond holding Judaism and Christianity together, is a force that pulls them strongly apart. If the canon is to be the central basis for faith, then it must be *either* the Jewish canon of the Hebrew Bible *or* the Christian canon of Old and New Testaments taken together. This opposition can, indeed, be reduced and something of the gulf overcome: but only if we do not stress the canon too heavily. In fact the God who emerges from the *Introduction* as the final perspective of the Old Testament is very much the unmoving, unchanging God of Judaism: it is a 'theocentric' religion with an eternal deity who has revealed his will unchangingly and from whom 'all causality ultimately derives'.[19] There is no sign here of a perspective that looks towards the God of Christianity, becoming incarnate at a certain point of time. The theocentric religion with its eternal deity is, of course, fully to be respected, and it may well be a right explication of what the canonizers may have thought. But it is not the God of Christians, or at most only partially so. In other words, the Old Testament has not been interpreted as *Christian* scripture after all. Perhaps the formal fact that both religions have a canon has been allowed to outweigh the fact that in terms of content and also of attitudes to scripture there are wide differences. The question of history comes into the matter also. A God who becomes incarnate is a God who has a history: an approach which seeks to reduce the theological relevance of history is one that will in the end emphasize unchanging eternity rather than change.

Here again we see a major difference from Barth. For Barth the strictly Christian doctrines, trinity and incarnation, were basic to any Old Testament interpretation. A Christian interpretation of Old Testament texts could not really agree with a Jewish interpretation. History (admittedly considerably redefined!) was essential to the understanding of God and of the Bible. The kind of Old Testament exegesis that Barth liked was the kind furnished by Wilhelm Vischer; when one no less than von Rad reviewed Vischer in a critical way, Barth told him that one could not criticize Vischer unless one first did even better than he.[20] An incarnate Christ in Genesis or in Joshua, yes; an unmoving eternal deity, from the viewpoint of Barth's sort of Christianity, no. The lines of development that led up to canonical criticism appear to differ in this respect from the finished product.

8. *Variations in canonical criticism.* In much that has been said I have spoken as if canonical criticism is one united position, but of

---

[19] Cf. *JSOT* 16, 1980, 22, where I make much the same point.
[20] See Barth, *KD* I/2, 87; *CD* I/2, 79f.

course it is not: it is more like a current of opinions running in roughly the same direction and containing certain recognizable elements of agreement as well as many differences. As has already been suggested, the ideas of the initial writings which got the movement under way were sometimes in effect abandoned in the realization, even by the same scholar. For instance, as has just been seen, Childs in an early article encouraged a sympathy for the sort of traditional exegesis in which the incarnate Christ is found throughout the pages of the Old Testament; but in his *Introduction* nothing on these lines is hinted at.

Another such difference attaches to the values of *description*. Much of the older biblical theology was deeply exercised by this question. Stendahl had urged that the first task of biblical theology was a descriptive one: to carry out an objective, historical description of the theology that lay within the Bible itself. To this then had to be added a second, more hermeneutic, approach, which would have the task of proceeding from 'what it meant' in the past to 'what it means' for the present.[21] Others, however, were deeply disturbed to find that the ideal of objective description was to be admitted at all. For many who were engaged in the older biblical theology, the idea of objective, descriptive study was very much to be deplored. In his article of 1964, which many have considered to be the starting point for the development of canonical criticism, Childs offers an interesting and promising new proposal. There was, it seemed, nothing wrong with description, the only question was of the object to be described. Past attempts had gone wrong because the object they had sought to describe was something like the historical development behind the text. But if the object to be described is the canon, such description could be welcomed warmly and positively. This suggestion necessarily meant that there was nothing wrong in the attitude of description as such, as many biblical theologians had thought: description is excellent, so long as it is the canon that is to be described. Traces of this can still be seen in Childs's *Introduction*: it 'seeks to describe as objectively as possible the canonical literature'.[22] So objective description is an entirely right attitude for the scholar. Clearly, therefore, it can never be right to criticize any scholarly endeavour on the ground that it follows the ideal of objective description. But it is doubtful whether this position is much upheld in canonical criticism as it has emerged. The *Exodus* commentary begins with a solemn declara-

---

[21] See Stendahl's article, 'Biblical Theology', in *IDB* i. 418–32, and my own with the same title in *IDB* supplementary vol., p. 106.
[22] Childs, *Introduction*, p. 16.

tion by the author that he 'does not share the hermeneutical position of those who suggest that biblical exegesis is an objective, descriptive enterprise'.[23] It is this latter position that has character-ized the enthusiasm for canonical criticism as a whole. Seen from that point of view, anyone professing to follow the ideal of objective description will be derided: by even setting up such an ideal he will be thought to have shown his complete lack of understanding of the nature of interpretation. Exactly this accusation is continually made against traditional biblical criticism; the anti-objectivist, anti-descriptivist rhetoric of much of the older biblical theology is taken up again.

This is an obvious confusion and canonical critics have not even tried to think straight on this theoretical issue. In many ways it does seem true that Childs's *Introduction* seriously seeks to implement the objective and descriptive ideal that he set himself. But why then should this fulfil the requirement to be 'theological', when other kinds of objective description seem not to do so? Because, perhaps, for Childs the canon is a holy object in itself, a sort of ikon: the merest descriptive tracing of its patterns is thus a sort of theological vision. Descriptive tracing of any other object, e.g. of salvation history or of the minds of the original writers, does not have this special status. The positive values of 'objective' and 'descriptive' when they are attached to the study of a central and controlling canon are values that are not shared by scholars who are taking some different approach. In other words, it is probable that 'objective' in Childs's usage here is equivocal: even his objective study could probably not be carried out except on the assumption of his own theological convictions, and he does not mean 'objective' to imply permission for other, quite different, approaches to the Bible to justify themselves as being objective. This again is reminiscent of the position in Barth and the Barthian tradition: objectivity is of the highest importance, but it derives only from proper recognition of the nature of the object; and it is Barthian theology (alone?) that has properly recognized this nature of the object, and therefore it only can be objective. The idea of objectivity does not allow different theologies to stand on equal terms of comparability; or, in other words, the word 'objectivity' is redefined so as to empty out its normal sense and make it so that only this particular theological conviction fulfils its sense. In any case, whatever the position of Barth, canonical criticism has been inconsistent in its attitude to the ideal of objective description. It has certainly forfeited the right to blame other sorts of scholarship for accepting that ideal.

[23] *Exodus*, p. xiii.

On one side, as many reviewers have thought, Childs's *Introduction*, however much thought out as objective description, reads very like a theology; and this may be a right reading, according to what has just been said. Provided it is focused upon the canon, objective description and theology merge into one. Not that necessarily theology would have nothing more to do: no doubt there would be many questions even after the *Introduction* has been absorbed. But it would have been already laid down that, in so far as any theology claimed to be biblical and to rest upon scripture, its entire approach to that material must be through the centrality of the canon. This prolegomenon seems to be the chief affirmation of theology.

Readers are justified, therefore, in asking what the actual content of the *Introduction* is. It is not at all clear that the objective description of the canonical shape of the books is that content. From one point of view, the real content is the theological vision of a theology for which the centrality of the canon is the single essential. From another, the real content is the drive to demolish what are believed to be the structures of traditional scholarship and replace them with something different. From another, the real content is not either theological or biblical, but more philosophical, the views about how the mind works and how scholarship works, the 'system of thought within which Childs is attempting to write an answer to a problem'.[24] The empirical material and analyses of the various Old Testament books are there to act as vehicle for the conveying of these truths. But for the insistent pressure of the conviction of these truths, it is doubtful whether the *Introduction* would have been written as it has. Naturally the presence of such strong convictions does not invalidate the presentation of material. But it remains a question whether the presentation of the material is so powerful as to constitute a confirmation of the assumptions under which it was written.

One brief example will show that in the detailed material also there have been differences between canonical criticism in its results and empirical studies which might have been expected to lead up to them. The *Introduction*, discussing the titles or superscriptions of the Psalms, says that these remove the Psalms from their older cultic context; they make them 'testify to all the common troubles and joys of ordinary human life', they move the emphasis to the inner life of the Psalmist and give an access to his emotional life. 'Far from tying these hymns to the ancient past, they have been contemporized and individualized for every generation of suffering and persecuted

---

[24] McEvenue, *Interpretation*, 35, 1981, 236.

Israel.'²⁵ But Childs himself had published, a decade earlier, an excellent study on these same titles: 'Psalm Titles and Midrashic Exegesis', *JSS* 16, 1971, 137–50. But this very fine article contains very little, in its more technical and detailed analysis, that can be said to foreshadow or to justify the interpretation offered in the *Introduction*.

Within canonical criticism different positions are held by Childs and by James A. Sanders. Something must be said about this difference too. Sanders's *Torah and Canon* (1972) began with 'A Call to Canonical Criticism' and in that sense may be regarded as the first full work in the genre. In a number of aspects Sanders's position is closer to that which I have taken. He rightly questions the idea that interpretation on the basis of what is claimed to be 'canonical context' really functioned in any community before the Reformation; he sees that there was an important shift in the mode of reading scripture—the shift, as he terms it, 'from that of story to that of oracle'—in the post-biblical period, and that a work like the Habakkuk Pesher had no interest whatever in reading according to canonical context; and he rightly sees that Childs contradicts himself by emphasizing the canonizing community but at the same time dissociating scripture from historical context. Moreover, he accepts the tradition of scholarship to a much greater degree than Childs and thus implies that any new departure, such as canonical criticism, will have to be an *addition* to existing procedures, or a complement to them, rather than an absolute revolution which will sweep them all away.²⁶ In these various respects the position here taken comes closer to the views of Sanders.

There are two respects, however, in which Sanders's position, even if in these respects more correct, seems to be less powerful and impressive, and thus less central as a subject for discussion, than the much more comprehensive work of Childs. The first is that his picture of the scholarly world and of the philosophical issues in knowledge seem to be again a mixture of the attitudes of the biblical theology movement and of those deriving from the more existential-ist strain of hermeneutics. Much of the rhetoric of these positions seems to be simply repeated. Consider this: 'Historical criticism in its handling of the Bible has by-passed the ancient communities which produced it and shaped it. It has focused, in good modern Western fashion, on individual authors.'²⁷ But this is entirely incorrect. I find it difficult to understand how scholars who have

²⁵ Childs, *Introduction*, p. 521, and cf. my remarks on this in *JSOT* 16, 1980, 19.
²⁶ All these can be found in *Horizons in Biblical Theology* 2, 1980, 188–91.
²⁷ Ibid., p. 183. Most criticism for most of this century has actually been community-centred rather than individual-centred: form criticism is the obvious example.

been so interested in a field like form criticism can say such a thing. Fragmentization of the text, creation of a gap between academic teaching and the work of the pastor, locking of the Bible into the past: these are simply the familiar assertions. There seems to be no fresh analysis of how scholarship works. This being so, it seems to be inadequate to counter the attacks of Childs by a confession of faith that biblical historical and literary criticism is a 'gift of God', as it assuredly is.[28] The positive vision of hermeneutics seems to depend very largely on vague wording and *non sequiturs*.[29]

Secondly, the actual handling of biblical evidence seems to me to be too speculative and too slight in substance to provide a solid framework for what is supposed to be a new movement in criticism. The point about the placing of Deuteronomy within the Torah, and the consequent separation between the Torah and the story thereafter, is, as already mentioned,[30] a point of importance; but it does not seem to me that *Torah and Canon* offers any other piece of evidence that has comparable solidity.

Too much seems to depend on very hypothetical arguments: if x had not happened, then how could y have happened, and if y did happen, how was it that z did not happen? Such arguments are not very compelling. Moreover, *Torah and Canon* is much too easy-going in reading into the biblical writers (or documents) its own modern hermeneutic ideas: 'the canonical prophets (the "true" prophets whose books we inherit) employed an existentialist hermeneutic which stressed neither continuity nor discontinuity but rather, on the basis of the Torah, raised the probing question as to Israel's true identity'.[31] I fully share Childs's doubts[32] about the importance here attached to concepts like 'identity' and to other categories like stability and adaptability. Nearly all the evidence cited in *Torah and Canon* seems to me to be susceptible of some different interpretation which in fact is not considered. The little book, though stimulating, does not form a sufficient basis for the starting point of canonical criticism at all.

This brings us to the last in our series of variations within canonical criticisms. It has generally been taken that Sanders's version of the new movement tries to concentrate on the process by which the canonical form is reached, a process from which he reconstructs the hermeneutic inherent in it, a hermeneutic which is then applicable to the church's modern need for understanding,

[28] Ibid., p. 192.
[29] Cf. *IDB* suppl. vol., s.v. 'Hermeneutics'.
[30] Cf. above, p. 51.
[31] *Torah and Canon*, p. 88.
[32] *Interpretation* 27, 1973, 88–91; also *Introduction*, p. 57.

while Childs is interested not in the *process* but in the canonical *text* itself, the text which results from the process. This seems to be the way in which they both understand their differences. But on Childs's side again we must note a discrepancy between theory and practice. His theoretical statements certainly emphasize the final text, the canonical form of the books. But the successive chapters of his *Introduction* are not in fact descriptions of the final text at all. They are much more descriptions of the way in which we, starting out from the results, antinomies, and failures of traditional scholarship, may find our way to the canonical form and its meaning. The will to describe the canonical form in itself has been subordinated to the will to show the deficiencies of traditional scholarship and the way in which, starting from it, we may pass to the canonical form. The effect of this is that Childs's *Introduction* is much less a meditation upon the canonical form than he thinks and much more a description of a *process* after all. As I previously wrote, 'For all his eulogies of the canonical form, Childs has not written a study of the canonical form after all.... In effect, the emphasis does not fall on the final form of the text: it falls on the historical joins which in the later stages led from the previous forms to the final text. And let us grant the importance of these joins. But—on the basis of the final text itself—these joins are less important than the content which lies between the joins.... The actual substance of most of the books stands out precisely because it is different from what the canonizers may have thought.'[33] Childs seems to me actually rather poor at realizing what the canonical form is like. A much truer description of canonical form would be produced if one simply forgot all about the defects of past scholarship, and about the community of canonizing times too, and indeed about the canon. Such a description would no doubt be a literary, perhaps structuralist, non-historical one; some might think it would not be theologically important either. But that seems to be the direction in which most of Childs's theoretical arguments lead, rather than the direction taken by his own *Introduction*.

9. *Literary aspects.* As has been remarked,[34] canonical criticism has a certain kinship with some movements in general literary appreciation and gains some of its attractiveness from that similarity. Conceptions of seeing a text as a whole, of reading it according to its own assumptions, of the irrelevance of previous forms of the text, of the 'intentional fallacy' of interpreting according to the intention of the author—all these have, however vaguely, contributed to the climate in which canonical criticism

---

[33] *JSOT* 16, 1980, 20f.   [34] Cf. above, p. 77.

became a possibility. In spite of this degree of support from literary theory, however, canonical criticism, at least in Childs's form, appears to be anxious to avoid becoming an essentially *literary* pursuit. Literature, after all, does not lead naturally to terms like *canon* and *authority* in the theological sense. For canonical criticism the Bible does not have the same kind of meaning as a play of Shakespeare or a poem of T.S. Eliot. Faced with the possibility of a really literary understanding, or of a structuralist approach, or of an interpretation like Ricoeur's in which 'the Bible is seen as a deposit of metaphors which contain inherent powers by which to interpret and order the present world of experience, regardless of the source of the imagery',[35] it flies back into a position surprisingly like that of the older biblical theology. Suddenly we find *history* being insisted on: the 'historical development of the biblical text', the 'historical context of the canonical text', the 'context of historic Israel', a 'historically-conditioned people of God'.[36] History, elsewhere so depreciated as a guide, suddenly and surprisingly comes in in order to safeguard canonical criticism from becoming a basically literary operation.

This caution is understandable; but one must wonder whether it is soundly based. Is it not the case that canonical criticism, if it can make something consistent out of its own principles, *should* accept that its natural direction leads towards identification with literary method? Not that this would make the Bible and its meaning just the same as any other literature and its meaning; the Bible would naturally be a special case, and always has been so in many ways. Moreover, canonical criticism would gain in theoretical strength and consistency by such a move. Any of these movements—modern literary theory, structuralism, Ricoeur's hermeneutics—is based on a far sounder philosophical foundation than the often muddled conceptual incoherence of canonical criticism. A really non-historical, literary study of the Bible on the basis of its shapes, styles and motifs could be very interesting. It would be much more original than canonical criticism, which is really still completely tied up in the inherited problems of theology. Instead of endlessly seeking to correct the older biblical scholarship, it could simply accept the latter as valid and go on its way in its own direction, taking or leaving as much of traditional scholarship as it needed. Authority, canon, relation to the community, origin in historic Israel, all the things that canonical criticism is interested in, could be slotted in as required with some redefinition. The logic of

---

[35] Childs, *Introduction*, p. 77.
[36] All phrases of Childs, ibid.

canonical criticism, and especially of its antipathy to older criticism and its historical interest, seems clearly to go in that direction.

But of course canonical critics are right to see that they cannot go far that way, because what they want is something theological, and they sense, I think rightly, that literary appreciation of the Bible and theological exegesis of it with authority for the church cannot be exactly the same thing, however much the former must illuminate the latter. But *why* are they not the same? One answer is to appeal to *history* as the essential context for theology, as Childs does in the passages just quoted: that is, the typical position taken by the older biblical theology. This seems to undermine the whole position of canonical criticism.[37] Or else one must answer that theology does not depend on the patterns of the Bible alone, but on the relations between the Bible and extra-biblical reality.[38] If that is so, canonical criticism alone can never be any more theological than any other kind of criticism: and, as we have seen, it is not.

Two or three other literary aspects remain to be mentioned:

Firstly, it is a *literary* question to what extent the editors of a biblical book, in putting together various sources or pieces of material, have created a meaning in the juxtaposition, as distinct from the meanings of the parts. 'The case for meaning must be decided on literary criteria: one must *show* that a unit is not just an anthology but is an intended structure with meaning.'[39] The fact that the book is canonized in this form or that does not in itself decide anything.

But, secondly, the question of meaning in these respects, as a literary question, has to be broadly historical at least, because we in our modern culture do not necessarily share, indeed do not normally share, the ancient cultural presuppositions which may be important for our deciding when elements and juxtapositions are meaningful and when they are fortuitous. A caution has here to be expressed about modern literary theory and its application to the Bible. Much modern literary theory seems to be built largely upon relatively modern literature, where the critic shares much more of the world of presuppositions of the literary works he is studying. Moreover, in the case of the Bible, much literary study sees the

[37] Perhaps Childs means that, though historical context is all-important, nothing useful can be achieved by actual historical investigation of it: if so, again a position familiar from the older biblical theology, and indeed from Barth.

[38] McEvenue, *Interpretation* 35, 1981, 236, writes: 'It is simply erroneous to think that one can proceed to truth of any kind using the Bible or a deposit of faith as the sole criterion. Unless you are simply restating the explicit biblical statement, you are always using some criterion outside the Bible.'

[39] McEvenue, ibid., p. 238.

Bible essentially through the eyes of its later readership, in medieval Christendom, in the Renaissance and Reformation, and in early modern times, and stresses the values and meanings seen in it during that time. But this approach, deeply impressive as it may well be, tends also to cover up the presuppositions and problems of the biblical situation itself.

If, however, we are interested in an analysis that depends on the presuppositions of biblical times themselves, then that carries us back to traditional historical-literary analysis. What a writer presupposed consisted of the beliefs that were already present in his mind before he formed the new text he was writing, and, in particular, the content of any previous writings of which he might know. We may therefore ask: when Gen. 2 was written, was the content of Gen. 1 among its presuppositions? or: when Gen. 1 was written, was the content of Gen. 2 among the presuppositions of the writer? In other words, we are back in traditional biblical criticism. It is a peculiar fact that the stress upon presuppositions has so often been deployed in modern discussion as if it was an argument *against* a historical approach: on the contrary, it is very obviously a strong support and justification for a historical approach. Obviously, also, it is a question exactly what the presuppositions of biblical men were, and the discussion and clarification of this is a matter for experts in various fields, who will probably have to draw much of their information from sources outside the biblical canon. The canonizers of both Old and New Testaments, in any case, certainly did not share the presuppositions of the writers of the earlier books within them.

Lastly, a word about 'canonical intentionality', which is one of Childs's rather mystic phrases: 'intentionality' is a term that belongs to historical reading, and thus, for example, it would apply if we were to read St. Paul in order to discover the *intention* which he as writer in his situation had. One of the ways to depreciate historical reading is to depreciate intentionality and say that we want to know not the intention of the writer but the meaning of the text.[40] This might be difficult with St. Paul—with whom it is always difficult to get away from the question of what he as writer actually intended—but could be readily understood with, say, St. John: if one asked him, 'What did you mean by your Gospel?' he might easily reply 'Never mind what I meant or intended: the Gospel *is* what I meant. It conveys its own meaning; I cannot usefully express a meaning, other than that indicated in these words.' This is at least what St. John *ought* to say if he had studied modern literary theory.

[40] Cf. my remarks in *JSOT* 16, 1980, 13f., and Childs, *Introduction*, pp. 79 etc.

In biblical studies, as we have seen, intentionality is a *critical* concept: it arises and becomes meaningful only when one no longer thinks of the Bible as a direct communication of true information from God.[41] It is often thought that biblical criticism tries to make people read the Bible *historically*. In some ways the reverse is true. In the seventeenth century, before criticism took hold, the Bible was very much a historical book and was to be read as such. A matter like the information that Methuselah lived for 969 years was simply a true fact.[42] It was correct historical information, absolutely true because given by God. Intentionality did not come into the question: the 'meaning' of the information was its correspondence with true fact. It was not biblical criticism that made the Bible into a historical book: rather, it was because the Bible was already believed to be a historical book that the study of it, under the pressure of critical theology, gradually led to biblical criticism. What applies to Methuselah applies to (say) the timing of the cleansing of the Temple in different Gospels: only when one sees that it is not a matter of exact fact does one begin to ask after the intention of the writer. Intention and intentionality are critical and developmental terms and belong to the set of ideas which Childs seeks to limit or expel. To attach them to the *canon* is contradictory; but it agrees with the observation that his approach to the canon is actually historical and developmental.

10. *History of the effects of biblical texts.* This subject is not directly a matter of canonical criticism but it has a connection and some remarks about it may be useful at this point. The Exodus commentary of Childs was an important stage in the development of canonical criticism and it contained considerable sections on the history of exegesis. The whole subject of *Wirkungsgeschichte* or history of effects has been much discussed elsewhere also. It is very true that the history of effects of texts has been neglected by much biblical criticism. There seem to be two questions: in what ways should this affect the future development of biblical studies, and how does it affect the practical design of works such as commentaries on biblical books?

Let us grant that biblical studies have concentrated too much on the concept of the 'original' and that more attention should be

---

[41] Cf. above, p. 122.

[42] For a literary disquisition on the highly interesting subject of Methuselah, the reader may be directed to the essay of Sir Thomas Browne, who seeks to show that it is a 'Vulgar and Common Error' to suppose 'that Methuselah must needs bee the longest liver of all the posterity of Adam': see his *Pseudodoxia Epidemica* or *Enquiries into Vulgar and Common Errors* (1646: ed. R. Robbins, Oxford University Press, 1981), pp. 542–4.

devoted to effects and less to origins. It is not clear, however, in what way this can be expected to alter the essential character of biblical criticism. No new conceptual tools, no alteration of investigative methods, appear to be necessary in order that the study of the history of effects should be undertaken. On the contrary, the recognition of the true history of effects is a highly *critical* task and expressly a historical-critical one. The more one emphasizes the history of effects, the more one emphasizes the historical investigation of a development. For the history of understanding cannot be discovered by simply looking at the texts: they themselves cannot tell us how they were later understood. In this respect the emphasis on history of effects must necessarily lead us away fom the emphasis on the canon: if we want to know how St. Paul was understood we have to read St. Ignatius, if we want to know the effects of Ezra and Nehemiah we have to read Ben Sira and Pirqe Aboth.

And this leads on to another point: the history of effects of texts cannot be studied unless we have *information*. Perhaps lack of such information was a reason why certain periods of the history of effects were not much studied. What pieces of information would the student be able to use in order to study the way in which books of the Bible were understood in the third century BC? If biblical scholarship was so blindly and dogmatically concentrated on *origins*, why was it that scholars fell with such enthusiasm and such overwhelming productivity on the Dead Sea Scrolls when they were discovered? Here again the writers we are reviewing have misdescribed modern biblical scholarship: the study of post-biblical interpretation in the form of the Scrolls has been a much livelier centre of activity since the war than traditional historical criticism has been.

The question of the organization of a commentary seems to be a different matter. A commentary is by its nature aligned with the sequence of the particular book being commented on; it is supposed to work from the literary linkages provided by that sequence. But biblical texts in their later effects, in the way they were used and understood in the later history of theology and devotion, entered into all sorts of new combinations and formed a network of meanings and patterns quite different from the constraints of their setting within that particular book. It thus seems to me almost impossible for a *commentary*, as a sequential exposition of a particular book, to follow out the effects of texts within these new networks. It is not necessarily *quite* impossible, but it is doubtful whether it is practicable. In fact attempts to follow this out in the setting of biblical commentaries often give only a selection of possibilities. In particular, it is important to observe that the commentary is not the main, nor even the principal, route through which biblical texts have had their effect: only in certain periods has the commentary been very important, and often the effect of biblical texts has travelled along other channels altogether. Therefore simply to consult and bring together the views of later *commentaries* is not necessarily to discover the most interesting things. Biblical texts had their effects in the minds and lives of scholars, theologians, and communities, all of whom were at the same time being affected by quite other considerations, coming from outside the biblical tradition: things like the fall of the Roman Empire, the Copernican Revolution, the discovery of Australia, and the rise of modern democracy. Thus anything said by any theologian or community about a particular text in Jeremiah or in St. John has to be integrated into a general view of what that theologian or community was thinking as a whole. In other words, the realities point, not towards an assemblage of later exegesis within the commentary on biblical books, but towards the already existing disciplines of patristics, historical theology, and church history. Commentaries that have sought to add material from the later history of exegesis are commonly liable to criticism, not simply because they have added all this material to the consideration of the biblical data itself, but because, having added so much, they have then left out so very much else that was equally relevant and could make much difference. The practical economy of scholarship suggests that the biblical commentary is not the best place to put all this material. All of it, incidentally, would have to be repeated endlessly, since much of what is relevant to one passage would be relevant to a hundred others.

One other point: if the history of exegesis is to be much more emphasized, and if it was neglected in the past, some of the blame for the neglect must go, not to the practice of biblical criticism, but to the traditional Protestant emphasis on the Bible as sole authority. The Bible could speak directly to each age, without the intervention of an authoritative tradition of exegesis. Long before biblical criticism arose, Protestant commentaries, though often heavily traditional, did not trouble much with the history of exegesis. This again has a moral for the total conception of biblical authority.

11. *Further assessments.* One of the problems with an essentially simple idea like that of canonical criticism is that it lumps together numerous quite different forces, all of which have only one common feature, namely that they are disliked by canonical criticism. Historical criticism is frequently opposed, because of its tendency to seek origins and its other harmful effects on ways of thinking about the Bible. But canonical criticism is also worried by

other harmful tendencies, such as the tendency to treat the Bible as if it was only a special example of ancient Near Eastern literature, or the interest in producing sociological or political interpretations of things in the Bible. With these, however, contradictory parameters are introduced. Study of the Bible as ancient Near Eastern literature is a very different thing from historical criticism. Indeed a great deal of that kind of study held itself very much apart from traditional biblical criticism during much of this century; on the whole, biblical criticism was fostered in theological faculties and taken very lightly by orientalists. More interaction between these two might have been creative. If some peculiar misunderstandings of the Bible came from orientalists, these might have been a good deal better if they had paid some attention to achievements in biblical criticism. Conversely, certain very unlikely theories of biblical criticism were modified and abandoned through the influence of oriental studies. The same applies to sociological explanations. Many of the uninformed sociological analyses of biblical matters would have been much more responsible if they had been informed by major trends of biblical criticism; some of them were probably motivated in the first place by the desire to avoid contact with these trends. Again, sociological explanations are not particularly historical nor are they necessarily origin-seeking. Thus what is said against a primarily *historical* analysis does not apply to them. Canonical criticism, at least in Childs's form, appears to be against these explanations not because they are historical but for a quite different reason, namely that they suggest that motives other than the purely religious went into the making of the Bible. Even theologically, however, that is a very unjustifiable opinion.

In spite of the enormous reading lavished by Childs on the history of scholarship and his wide knowledge of the field, his picture of the scene of scholarship in the last decades must be pronounced highly distorted. The supposed dominance of historical criticism, of orientalism, of sociological and other approaches can hardly count in the balance against the amount of energy and productivity that has gone, and goes, into the theologically-conscious interpretation of the Bible. And the theological achievement of these decades has been enormous; and very little of it is in fact vitiated by the effects of these malevolent influences. If modern biblical scholarship has failed, in spite of people like Eichrodt and von Rad, to satisfy, the reason lies not in their acceptance of these influences but in problems and tensions within the world of theology itself. For theology is not agreed within itself. Under the surface canonical criticism is perhaps a way of promulgating yet another theology.

But why should we accept that other theology? Childs seems to think that his position about the canon is part of the Christian faith. It is 'the church's confession of the canon'. But the church does not 'confess' the canon in that sense, and it certainly does not 'confess' all the intellectual paraphernalia of canonical criticism. The canon as such is not directly a matter of the church's 'confession' and never has been so in any form of Christianity. Scripture certainly comes into the church's confession, but that confession is not *of* scripture: it is of persons and events that are known and understood '*according to* the scriptures'. The scriptures themselves are not the subject of 'confession', and the canon still less.[43] What canonical criticism seems to have done is to create a pseudo-traditional theology in order to solve problems and antinomies of biblical scholarship.

In terms of the distinction mentioned above,[44] the conceptions of canonical criticism appear to be very much *deductive* in character. Given the fact that there is a canon, one may deduce from it that, since it is a matter of form, its form must be all-important—for, if its form were different, one might deduce that its meaning would be different; and, since the form is all-important, one may go on to deduce that the canon must be the controlling force in all interpretations. Canonical criticism is the elaborate academic enterprise of marshalling the biblical material in such a way as to show that it conforms to this ideal. But what if there were also *other* all-important influences? There cannot be, for the canon implies— deductively--that there cannot be any which could infringe upon the governing position of the canon.

But against this there stands the *inductive* fact of scriptural evidence, in point of content, suggesting that no one in biblical times, or at best only a few, actually drew the conclusions that these deductions require, and that their attitude to the canon was something quite different. And this is not true of the men of the Bible only: it was probably true of most later ages also. Even for the later ages the attitudes actually held have to be discovered from actual evidence, not by reasoning from the concept of the canon. As stated above,[45] even in Protestant orthodoxy the church did not focus its attention evenly upon the canon of scripture: for its veneration was attached also to the persons and events known therein.

One more word about biblical theology. Canonical criticism was launched with the claim that it would lead to a new biblical theology. But one has to ask whether this is so great an advantage.

---

[43] Cf. the statement of Berkhof cited above, p. 48n.
[44] Cf. above, p. 22.   [45] Cf. above, p. 4.

There are good theological reasons for supposing that biblical theology, even if justifiable and necessary, should not be allowed to determine the shape or the decisions of theology as a whole. Theology as a whole has its right to decide differently from whatever biblical theology may offer as its results. It therefore is not inevitable that the presentation of the material in the form of a biblical theology should be the most favourable mode in which biblical studies can provide data for theological evaluation. The ideal that biblical studies should always be as theologically minded as possible is not necessarily the best thing for theology itself. It may well be that biblical studies do a greater service for theology by their sequential commentaries, by their historical work, and by their illumination of the situation and the mind of the original writers than they can perform through any other mode. I do not say that I actually think this: I have already said that I consider biblical theology to have a useful function to perform. I merely suggest that the maximum benefit for theology is a question for theology itself to consider and determine, and cannot be pre-empted by erecting yet another sort of system claiming to be biblical theology. The particular system of canonical criticism is, however, unlike all previous forms of biblical theology in the degree of its determination to prevent theology obtaining from biblical scholarship just the sort of knowledge that it may, after all, find most desirable, and most beyond its own power to provide. For theologians, after all, if they want to be governed by the shape of the canon, have the power to decide that for themselves; they do not need the entire apparatus of biblical scholarship employed to tell them only that.

Consider also this further aspect. It is not easy for any modern exegetical approach to establish congruence with older traditions of interpretation. We may establish a likeness in one respect, only to find that a new divergence has been created in another aspect of which we had not thought at all. In much 'pre-critical' exegesis the Bible stood apart from other sources of truth because its truth was divinely guaranteed and therefore absolute, and because it functioned in the life and liturgy of the church. But because it was truth it was not separated from all other truth. Knowledge of ancient history or of philosophy did not have the same divine guarantees of truth: but where they were true they had truth of the same kind as the truth that the Bible furnished. Extra-biblical truth was valued very highly in the older theological tradition of the church. Ancient history and philosophy in particular were deeply involved in theological thinking. There was nothing like as much of this extra-biblical knowledge as there is today; but they would have longed for more, if they could have had it. That which was true, because known from the Bible, formed a unitary world-view with that which was true because known from other sources. The fact that both were true guaranteed this. The character of the Bible as a limited corpus did not cut it off in terms of the *kind* of knowledge from what was otherwise known to be true.

In other words, the sophisticated attempts to separate off the Bible from other sources of knowledge through establishing it as a separate cognitive zone, governed by different rules of understanding, are a modern and—I think—a twentieth-century innovation. They are a response to the fact that extra-biblical knowledge has become so great and its effects—at least to some—unwelcome. Barth's thought is one outstanding effort to deal with this problem. The older biblical theology was a very obvious case: many of its manifestations sought to establish the existence of a special biblical cognition, a biblical logic, which would make it clear that the comprehension of the Bible followed different principles from those to be found elsewhere. The Bible could be seen, therefore, as a closed system with its own interconnections, which have to be seen in their own way and form a quite different profile from the contours of other forms of knowledge. And I do not necessarily say that this is wrong: there are problems in the Bible which may well deserve to be handled in this way. Canonical criticism seems to be another attempt to do this same thing but in a different way: instead of establishing the separateness of biblical truth through biblical logic or thought patterns, it seeks to do it through the separation constituted by the canon, which establishes the Bible as a distinct and independent cognitive unit. But all this is distinctly modern and creates quite a different gulf of distance from older interpretative tradition. In spite of its sympathy for older exegesis, canonical criticism, by making the Bible into an intellectual ghetto separated from all other truth by the walls of relevance, is creating just as serious a break from older exegesis as historical criticism did.

12. *Conclusion.* Canonical critics have sometimes argued that the older biblical criticism posed its questions in too simple a way: historical questions, in particular, were too simple to deal with the complexity of the material. The reverse is true. Historical questions are of immense complexity. If the questions put are excessively simple, the obvious way to deal with it is to recall the critics to the complexity of their own business. Or it may be that, in dealing with an ancient situation where there is little information other than the Bible itself, over-simple questions and answers are the only ones possible. In fact it is canonical criticism that is simplistic. Basically it has only one idea: the controlling place of the canon. To others this may fall apart into several conflicting ideas, but to the canonical

critic himself it is all one idea. There is of course complexity even in the canon, but all that complexity can be dealt with by the one simple idea. It is simple because no other principle is to be allowed to interfere with it, and it is of such a nature that it rules out other sorts of knowledge as irrelevant. This probably accords with much popular religious sentiment: biblical studies are hideously complex, they require technical expertise, they are full of divergent sources, periods, and hypotheses: the canonical principle leaves the believer at peace, alone with his Bible.

Actually, however, as we have suggested, the canonical principle on analysis falls apart into several quite different and sometimes conflicting sets of ideas. It is therefore not easy to give an answer to the question, what sort of future there is for canonical criticism and in what ways it may be expected to develop. Moreover, even if most of what has been written as canonical criticism so far is wrong, one might still ask the question whether the subject in itself might still be worthy of pursuit, with some changes in method. I agree with McEvenue that the canonical principle as it at present stands is a myth, a beautiful biblical myth.[46] Nevertheless it may have valuable suggestions to offer.

Much of the best detailed biblical work presented by canonical criticism has in fact been literary-historical criticism, differing from traditional scholarship in focus, aspect, and interest. The natural positive return one could expect from this would be an improvement in the modes of literary-historical reading. For example, historical study has too often acted as if the diachronic study of change is the first and only step. Against this it could well be urged that the synchronic study of documents and social states logically precedes, rather than follows, the diachronic study of change. This might well be a natural corrective that would arise from the concerns of canonical criticism. It cannot well be fruitful, however, so long as the anti-historical bias of much of the latter is maintained.

The emphasis on the final stage of the text is, naturally, also interesting; but in itself it is not so very important. If pressed far enough, it ought to lead to something like a non-historical, structural, literary reading. When one comes to questions of detailed meaning, semantic value of linguistic items, likely presuppositions, questions of against what opposing force the passage is written, and the like, it would break down. Over many questions one would simply have to say one did not know what the text could mean. For theology and preaching, states of the text previous to the

[46] *Interpretation* 35, 1981, 237.

final are certainly legitimate. In any case the final state of the text, applying as it does to individual books by contrast with previous sources or forms, is substantially different from the canon.

The stress on the history of exegesis is entirely wholesome; but it again is a matter of historical reading. It depends on the sources that are available. If it is a history after biblical times, then the sources have to be read historically; if it is an inner-biblical sort of historical criticism, then it is a special case of ordinary biblical criticism. If it is the post-biblical exegesis, it leads away from the canon: it is now a matter of patristic or later theology. This subject is well served by the disciplines which study it.

The idea that the biblical material was always, throughout its main development, in a sense 'canonical', in that traditions were selected and preserved because they were recognized as authoritative, is highly probable, but is not essentially different from what has been always supposed. Only historical research could tell us what this 'pre-canon' contained at any particular time. The more the 'pre-canon' is emphasized, the less the final form of the text can be stressed.

The claim that canonical criticism can lead to a more theological form of biblical studies must be considered unlikely. It is difficult to see how any possible product arising from it could be *more* theological than the biblical study of the era of Cullmann and von Rad, Hoskyns and Davey and Alan Richardson. What might emerge is the following: on the one side a useful description of the canonical literature as it stands, which might serve helpfully for the appreciation of the Bible as literature, in other words, for a rather non-theological purpose; on the other side an account of the dynamics and development of the canon and of canonical form, which would serve as preparatory material for theological evaluation; the theological evaluation, however, would have to handle the canonical material thus described in a critical and evaluative way, that is, it would not be constrained to follow the lines of the canon as described.

The first necessity for progress with the heritage of canonical criticism, if such progress is to be made, is, however, to revise the peculiar picture of modern biblical scholarship upon which it so often depends. I have suggested that this picture is a stereotype inherited from the older biblical theology and reinforced by the hermeneutical discussions. In the forties, when biblical theology, in that sense of the word, began, there was some justification for that picture. There were then some scholars for whom source analysis and the dating of authors were the whole of knowledge, for whom there was no room at all for biblical theology, for whom extra-biblical parallels or evolutionary development seemed as important as the contents of the Bible itself. Even for that time this may be an exaggeration. But to look on the scholarship of the sixties, seventies, and eighties as if it fitted that pattern is very strange. How did Cullmann and von Rad and others manage to write any biblical theology, if they were so encumbered by the assumptions of historical criticism? In fact they proved that the full acceptance of historical criticism formed no sort of barrier to the production of highly impressive works of biblical theology.[47] The facts are the reverse of the picture we have been considering. Our generation is one that grew up not under the dominion of historical criticism, but much too much under the dominion of the assumptions of biblical theology; it is out of these assumptions that it had to find its way. This does not imply that there is anything necessarily wrong about biblical theology; it remains a mere fact that it was for many the dominating intellectual force. This means, however, that its picture of the intellectual heritage which it took over can no longer be valid or useful for the generation which took over its heritage. Much of this question, in other words, is about the diagnosis and understanding of the intellectual character of scholarship. For that reason it has been necessary to go far back and to ask questions about the nature of biblical criticism and its whole relation to the theological history of modern times, as well as to the contacts it has with other disciplines.

---

[47] It was those who rejected historical criticism who showed themselves unable to write any worthwhile biblical theology.

Abbreviations

CD	*Church Dogmatics* (K. Barth)
E.T.	English Translation
IDB	*Interpreter's Dictionary of the Bible*
KD	*Kirchliche Dogmatik* (K. Barth)
JBL	*Journal of Biblical Literature*
JSOT	*Journal for the Study of the Old Testament*
JSS	*Journal of Semitic Studies*
JTS	*Journal of Theological Studies*
ZAW	*Zeitschrift für die Alttestamentliche Wissenschaft*

Bibliography

THIS bibliography is divided into two sections. The first lists works that are specially relevant for the recent discussion of the canon and canonical criticism. These are separated out, with the idea that they might form a helpful tentative reading list for anyone wishing to study the literature of this recent movement. The second section lists other works that are mentioned in the present book.

I. WORKS OF RECENT DISCUSSION ON CANON AND CANONICAL CRITICISM

ANDERSON, B.W. 'Tradition and Scripture in the Community of Faith', *JBL* 100, 1981, 5–21

BLENKINSOPP, J. *Prophecy and Canon* (Notre Dame, Indiana: Notre Dame Press, 1977)

CAMPENHAUSEN, H. VON, *The Formation of the Christian Bible* (London: A. & C. Black, 1972)

CHILDS, B.S. 'Interpretation in Faith', *Interpretation* 18, 1964, 434ff.

—*Biblical Theology in Crisis* (here abbreviated as *Crisis*; Philadelphia: Westminster Press, 1970)

—'The Old Testament as Scripture of the Church', *Concordia Theological Monthly*, 43, 1972, 709–22

—*Exodus* (London: SCM Press, 1974)

—'The 'Sensus Literalis of Scripture: an Ancient and Modern Problem', in *Beiträge zur alttestamentlichen Theologie* (Zimmerli Festschrift); Göttingen: Vandenhoeck and Ruprecht, 1977), 80–93

—'The Exegetical Significance of Canon for the Study of the Old Testament', in *Vetus Testamentum* Supplements 29 (Göttingen Congress Volume; Leiden: E.J. Brill, 1978), 66–80

—'The Canonical Shape of the Prophetic Literature', *Interpretation* 32, 1978, 46–55

—*Introduction to the Old Testament as Scripture* (London: SCM Press, 1979)
Major reviews of the *Introduction* include: *JSOT* 16, 1980, with reviews by B. Kittel, J. Barr, J. Blenkinsopp, H. Cazelles, G.M.M. Landes, R.E. Murphy, R. Smend, and response by Childs; *Horizons in Biblical Theology* (Pittsburgh), 2, 1980, 113–211, with reviews by B.C. Birch, D.A. Knight, J.L. Mays, D.P. Polk, and J.A. Sanders, and response by Childs. Cf. also reviews by:
W. Harrelson, *JBL* 100, 1981, 99–103
S. McEvenue, 'The Old Testament, Scripture or Theology?', *Interpretation* 35, 1981, 229–42
J.G. Janzen, *Interpretation* 34, 1980, 411–14
R. Murray, *Heythrop Journal* 22, 1981, 442–4

COATS, G.W. AND LONG, B.O. *Canon and Authority* (Philadelphia: Fortress Press, 1977)

FREEDMAN, D.N. 'Canon of the OT', in *IDB* Supplementary Volume (Nashville: Abingdon, 1976), 130–6

KÄSEMANN, E., ED. *Das Neue Testament als Kanon* (Göttingen: Vandenhoeck and Ruprecht, 1970)

LEIMAN, S. *The Canonization of Hebrew Scripture* (Hamden, Connecticut; Archon Books, 1976)

PFEIFFER, R.H. 'Canon of the OT', *IDB* i. 498–520 (Nashville: Abingdon, 1962)

SANDERS, J.A. *Torah and Canon* (Philadelphia: Fortress Press, 1972); see also under Childs and under Coats and Long

—'Hermeneutics', *IDB* Supplementary Volume (Nashville: Abingdon, 1976), 402–7

SPINA, F.A. 'Canonical criticism: Childs versus Sanders', *Interpreting God's Word For Today* (Wesleyan Theological Perspectives, 2; Anderson, Indiana: Warner Press, 1982), pp. 165–94.

SUNDBERG, A.C. *The Old Testament of the early Church* (Harvard Theological Studies 20, 1964)

—'Canon of the NT', *IDB* Supplementary Volume (Nashville: Abingdon, 1976), 136–40

II. OTHER WORKS REFERRED TO

ABRAHAM, W.J. *The Divine Inspiration of Holy Scripture* (Oxford: Oxford University Press, 1981)

BARR, JAMES *Old and New in Interpretation* (London: SCM Press, and New York: Harper and Row, 1966; 2nd edn., London, 1982)

—'The Old Testament and the New Crisis of Biblical Authority', *Interpretation* 25, 1971, 24–40

—*The Bible in the Modern World* (London: SCM Press, and New York: Harper and Row, 1973)

—'Trends and Prospects in Biblical Theology', in *JTS* 25, 1974, 265–82

—'Story and History in Biblical Theology', in *Journal of Religion* 56, 1976, 1–17

—'Biblical Theology', 'Revelation in History', and 'Scripture, Authority of', in *IDB* Supplementary Volume (Nashville: Abingdon, 1976), 104–11, 746–9, 794–7

—*Fundamentalism* (London: SCM Press, 2nd edn., 1981, and Philadelphia: Westminster, 1978)

—Review of D.H. Kelsey, *The Uses of Scripture in Recent Theology*, in *Virginia Seminary Journal* 30.3 and 31.1 (Alexandria, Virginia), 1978–9, 39f.

—Review of Childs, *Introduction, JSOT* 16, 1980, 12–23

—*Explorations in Theology 7* (London: SCM Press, 1980; Philadelphia: Westminster, 1980 under the title *The Scope and Authority of the Bible*)

—'Bibelkritik als theologische Aufklärung', in T. Rendtorff, *Glaube und Toleranz. Das theologische Erbe der Aufklärung* (forthcoming)

—'Jowett and the Reading of the Bible "like any other book"', in *Horizons in Biblical Theology* 1982–3

BERKHOF, H. *Christian Faith* (Grand Rapids: Eerdmans, 1979); Dutch original *Christelijk Geloof* (Nijkerk: Callenbach, 1973)

BROWNE, SIR THOMAS *Pseudodoxia Epidemica* (Oxford: ed. R. Robbins, Oxford University Press, 1981)

COGGINS, R.J. *Samaritans and Jews* (Oxford: Blackwell, 1975)

EISSFELDT, O. *The Old Testament* (Oxford: Blackwell, 1965)

EVANS, R.J.W. *The Making of the Habsburg Monarchy* (Oxford: Clarendon Press, 1979)

GERHARDSSON, B. *Memory and Manuscript* (Lund: Gleerup, 1961)

HENRY, P. *New Directions in New Testament Study* (Philadelphia: Westminster, 1979)

HORNIG, G. *Die Anfänge der historisch-kritischen Theologie* (Göttingen: Vandenhoeck and Ruprecht, 1961)

JONES, D. 'The Traditio of the Oracles of Isaiah of Jerusalem', in *ZAW* 67, 1955, 226–46

KELSEY, D.H. *The Uses of Scripture in Recent Theology* (London: SCM Press, and Philadelphia: Fortress Press, 1975)

LAMPE, G.W.H. *A Patristic Greek Lexicon* (Oxford: Clarendon Press, 1961)

MAIER, G. *The End of the Historical-critical Method* (St. Louis: Concordia, 1977)

POLZIN, R.M. *Biblical Structuralism* (Philadelphia: Fortress Press, and Missoula, Montana, Scholars Press, 1977)

PUMMER, R. 'The Present State of Samaritan Studies', *JSS* 21, 1976, 39–61; 22, 1977, 27–47

REVENTLOW, H. *Bibelautorität und Geist der Moderne: die Bedeutung des Bibelverständnisses für die geistesgeschichtliche und politische Entwicklung in England von der Reformation bis zur Aufklärung* (Göttingen: Vandenhoeck und Ruprecht, 1980)

RICOEUR, P. *Essays on Biblical Interpretation* (Philadelphia: Fortress Press, 1980; London: SPCK, 1981)

SAWYER, J.F.A. *Semantics in Biblical Research* (London: SCM Press, 1972)

SMART, J.D. *The Past, Present and Future of Biblical Theology* (Philadelphia: Westminster, 1979)

SPARKS, H.F.D. 'Jerome as Biblical Scholar', *Cambridge History of the Bible* (Cambridge: Cambridge University Press, 1970), i. 510–40

STUHLMACHER, P. *Historical Criticism and Theological Interpretation of Scripture* (British edition with Introduction by J. Barr, London: SPCK, 1979)

WINK, W. *The Bible in Human Transformation* (Philadelphia: Fortress Press, 1973)

Index of Names and Subjects

Index of Biblical Passages

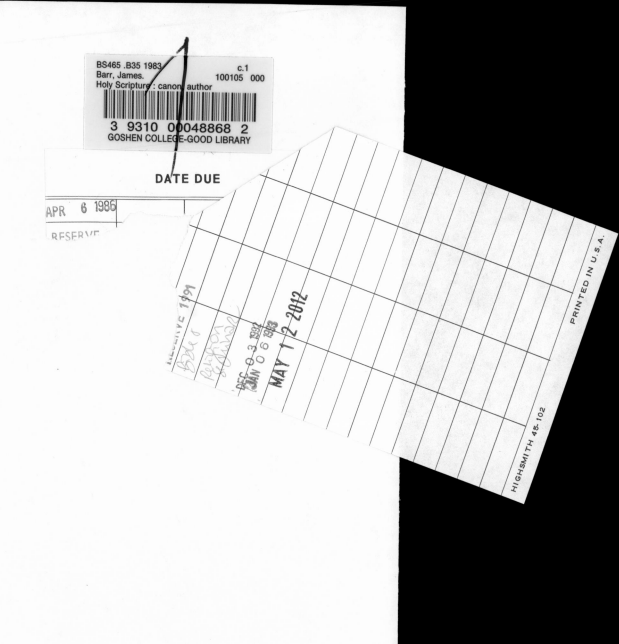